It was winter. Carola and I were sitting in a bay window of the house we were living in at the time, staring through the leaded casement windows at the snow outside.

"What's the use of going on?" she queried.

"Going on with what?"

"Oh, life, marriage, everything," she sighed.

"What's the matter?"

"Good grief, can't you tell? How could you ask such a question? I'm depressed. I feel useless. I can't stand the children; the house is a mess except when Rosa picks up; and you're so remote and self-satisfied I can never get you to face the truth."

L. Ld
11-3-07

THE EYE OF THE STORM

Joseph P. Bishop

BETHANY HOUSE PUBLISHERS
MINNEAPOLIS, MINNESOTA 55438
A Division of Bethany Fellowship, Inc.

The verses on page 96 are from POEMS by Emily Dickenson, Edited by Martha Dickenson Bianchi and Alfred Leete Hampson, and published by Little, Brown and Company.

Originally published by Chosen Books

The Eye of the Storm
Joseph P. Bishop

ISBN 0-87123-263-4

Published by Bethany House Publishers
A Division of Bethany Fellowship, Inc.
6820 Auto Club Road, Minneapolis, Minnesota 55438

Printed in the United States of America

TO
two great congregations,
one in Swarthmore, Pennsylvania,
and one in Rye, New York—
they bore my pain and failure with love

Preface

In August 1954 we were at our summer home in Rhode Island when a hurricane hit the eastern seaboard. With almost contemptuous strength the wind picked up beach houses and tossed them like match boxes half a mile inland. Together my wife, Carola, our children and I stood at the living-room window watching the pounding ocean slice a new breachway through the sandbar on the other side of our saltwater pond. The level of the pond rose before our eyes, a foot every minute, threatening to march right up the hill on which our house stood. The electric power to the house had long since been cut, and so presently I fought through the storm out to the automobile to listen to the local radio station. The announcer's disciplined voice was reassuring: "We are at present experiencing the worst of the storm. If you are on high ground, stay where you are."

I switched off the radio and was starting my dash back to the house when an amazing thing occurred. That humid, hot, irresistible wind suddenly and astonishingly stopped.

I knew that all around me was raging a storm of unimaginable destructiveness. But where I stood, at the very center of all that violence, not a twig moved, not a blade of grass stirred. An immense calm had settled over our house and yard, and as long as we remained in the eye of the storm, not a breath of the disturbance all around got to us.

I have thought of that experience often in the years since, as other, more personal, storms have buffeted me. I write about two of them in this book: the first a sudden bereavement, when our son was killed "all out of season" in an automobile accident; the second, Carola's protracted struggle with cancer. But what I learned in these two—alas!— not uncommon crises, holds true I think for all human need. The answer to life's traumas is not to be found in escape and denial, but in the center of the problem itself. The peace of God is discovered in the eye of the storm.

Years ago, before Peter's death, before Carola's illness, I wrote a small article for *Guideposts* magazine titled, "The Way Out Is the Way Through." "The answer to any human dilemma," I said, "is never to slip out the side exit. It is not to run out the back door. The way out of trouble, grief, frustration, even personal disaster is to come face-to-face with the matter at hand and go on through to the other side.

"The reason the way out is the way through is that God's power is available to us only at the point of faith, not at the point of fear and timidity. The truth is that those who flee reality also are fleeing God and the help He might have given them."

Little did I think when I wrote those words how soon I was to test them. At the time I was speaking as a pastor who has always loved his congregations extravagantly and felt their sorrows as his own. I applied them to a man with a job problem, to a wife about to leave her husband, to a widower who no longer wanted to go on living. I am grateful to the insights granted me by all these people; today, however, I have experienced so much more of the truth of those words, it is like the difference between a pond and the ocean.

RYE, NEW YORK
MARCH, 1976

Acknowledgments

We are all debtors to one another, but in writing this book I am especially indebted to Elizabeth Sherrill whose editing of my manuscript was like taking a winding, circuitous road and making it straight. For her encouragement, faith and sensitive skill I am deeply grateful.

I wish also to acknowledge with gratitude my debt to a longtime friend, Dorothy Cogswell, now in her declining eighties, whose kindness through deep waters preserved my dignity and my hope. My warm appreciation, too, needs to be expressed to Catherine Marshall, Leonard LeSourd and John Sherrill whose faith that this book needed to be published has made it possible; and finally my thanks to Barbara Ferguson for her typing skills, her patience and her trust.

THE EYE
OF THE STORM

1

It was 5:35 in the morning of an August Sunday in 1965. The telephone downstairs in our summer house in Rhode Island was ringing, unnaturally loud in the early-morning stillness.

Barefooted, I groped down the stairs and into the pantry. Over the phone a man's voice: "This is the New Hampshire State Police." The tone was abrupt, almost accusing. "Do you know Peter Bishop?"

"He's our son," I replied, suddenly wide awake, wondering what possible trouble the boy could have gotten into.

"He was killed in an automobile accident last night," the remorseless voice continued. "The body's at the Laconia General Hospital. You'll have to come up to identify him."

As I put the phone back on its cradle, grief literally bent me double. I was dimly aware of my wife Carola at my side. I had not heard her come down the stairs. Through my uncontrollable sobbing I told her what the police officer had said. For a while she did not speak, then quietly—so quietly—she began asking questions. "How did it happen? What time did it happen? Was Peter driving? Was he killed right away? Was anyone else hurt?"

Of course I didn't know the answers. A wild irrational anger rose in me that she was asking questions while I was stunned with the crushing single fact that Peter was dead at seventeen. Later, of course, I understood that this was her way of laying hold of the ungraspable: to come at it piecemeal, in mind-sized facts—while I let the full impact overwhelm me at once.

Somehow we had gotten into the living room. The sun had already risen on a calm summer sea. I looked down at the dock through the large front window, and there was the beetle catboat the boy loved to sail. I could see his face as he sat in the stern, tiller in one hand, sheet in the other, his large blue eyes bright with excitement before the wind, his mouth set in a slightly diagonal line of anxious resolution.

The thing was more than I could manage. My outcry waked Holly. Our eldest child and our only girl, Holly was just home from her counselor's job at a camp in Maine; in a few weeks she'd be entering her junior year at Radcliffe College. As Holly came downstairs I heard Carola's voice, still so terribly quiet: "Peter's been killed in an automobile accident, Holly-bird. That's all we know."

The three of us held one another close, there in our pajamas that Sunday morning. After awhile I composed myself enough to accompany Carola upstairs to tell the other two children.

Both boys, Timothy, fifteen, and Morin, twelve, were sitting up in their beds in the room they shared together. Carola and I took them in our arms. I still couldn't speak. Carola had to say the words. "We are sorry, darlings, to have to tell you that Peter has gone to his heavenly home. He died last night in an automobile accident."

Timmy's eyes grew large. Morin clung to my neck. I explained that I had to go to Laconia to make various arrangements.

Presently, I was dressed and shaved. Carola and I thought it best that she remain with the children. So I set off alone, a little before seven in the morning, to find the Laconia General Hospital, about 150 miles north.

I'd been driving for an hour when, passing through a small village, I was stopped by a red light. As I waited for it to turn, I noticed a small gray-stone church on the corner. At that very minute the bell in the tower began to ring.

At once I knew the summons was for me. I said to myself, "There is nothing you can do now for Peter. There is no rush. And if you are going to get through this, you will have to find a strength which is greater than your own." Thank God for the blessed pauses of life.

It was a simple Gothic-style church, seating not more than 150. I knelt to pray: "Dear God, you know I am not asking questions about why or how this could happen to me; but one thing I do ask, and I ask it with all my being, give me some sign that you are real. More than anything, I need to know that you are real."

Presently, the service began. Scripture has always been to me a source of meaning deeper than any other writing;

and so the natural place for me to expect an answer to my prayer was when the Bible lessons were read. Soon I was listening to the passage from First Corinthians which concludes with these words, "This suffering which has come to you is none other than that which is common to all men. God is faithful, and He will not permit you to be tested above that which you are able to bear."

Then followed the Gospel lesson, which that day was Jesus' parable of the prodigal son. Our son was no prodigal. The joy and satisfaction he gave to us was so consistent and abundant that we used to say, "He's almost too good to be true." That morning, however, I heard only the shining central story: that a beloved son had come back to the Heavenly Father's home. The father's words about the son seemed spoken straight to me, "He was dead, and is now alive."

I dropped to my knees again in the pew to say, "Thank you, God. I am a sinful and stubborn man, but I am not deaf. Thank you for answering my prayer. I hear you, and I know 'Thou art.' That's all I need to know."

After I had received the sacrament, I left the church with gratitude, got into my car and continued the trip, not without intense pain and anguish, but aware also of a kind of strength flooding into me from a depth I had not known was there.

Grief is a private kind of pain, each loss in life bringing its own shape and texture; but in whatever form, if it is given its way for a season amid solitude and silence, it has great restorative power. It can, of course, be disguised as anger and guilt, or it can bear down on the heart with its awful weight until it crushes us. As long as we refuse to drink the cup of grief, we are doomed to carry it in some such destructive fashion, but if we can, by some grace, accept it, grief can begin to work its healing in us.

The way out of heartbreak, as out of every storm of human existence, is always and only the way through the center. We cannot cover this distance all at once, of course, but we can take the first step. We can start by saying to ourselves with integrity, "This has happened to thousands of others." This suffering which has come to you is none other than that which is common to all men. Accept it as part of life's unlimited possibility. Don't resist the invitation to join the ranks of those who have walked through just such suffering as this. Their company will bless you and awaken in you a new sense of belonging to the human family; and if you will walk through it, not around it, there is blessedness at the end of the tunnel.

The Laconia General Hospital was not difficult to find. As I drove into the parking lot, I found Paul Abry waiting for me. Paul was the chaplain of the Groton School where Peter was to have entered his senior year the next month. Peter loved him as I did. He was a warm, compassionate, hulky kind of man, with a florid complexion, bushy eyebrows, and a full head of hair. He was sitting on the front steps of the hospital, head bowed, smoking a cigarette. He saw me walking toward him and got up, tossing the cigarette away.

"I'm so sorry, Joe; I'm so terribly, terribly sorry!"

Peter had been working that summer for Paul in a camp operated by the Groton School for disadvantaged children of Boston. He had enjoyed the work and the youngsters had enjoyed him, whether it was on the playing fields or with his guitar perched on his knees singing the plaintive songs of the sixties.

"How did it happen?" I asked Paul as we stood there in the glaring noonday sun.

"We had closed up the camp, stored all the gear," Paul began, "and as you know, Peter planned to rejoin you and the family in Rhode Island today.

"He and three other kids decided to drive into town last night for a movie. There wasn't any liquor involved—the police were very clear on that. They were on their way back to camp when Pete's VW hit a soft shoulder, and before he could get it under control his side of the car hit a tree.

"The other kids are okay. They walked away from the accident and got help from a nearby house. The ambulance came and Pete was admitted to the hospital at 11:45 last night. No one got in touch with me until 4 A.M., and that's when I told them to call you in Rhode Island."

It was clear to me that Paul had rehearsed these words many times. He said them almost as though he were hypnotized. His shock was terrible to see. I clasped his hands and said gently, "It's all right, Paul. These things happen. I don't know why I should be spared. Wait for me here, while I find the boy."

Inside the hospital I was directed to the emergency room. The nurse told me the name of the doctor who had operated on Peter and said he was presently in the building. Someone found him and brought him to me where I was sitting on a bench in the corridor.

The young man's eyes blazed when he saw me, "Don't

you people in New York require seat belts? I use one all the time. That boy of yours might be alive today if he had used a seat belt."

"Doctor, how did Peter die?"

"A massive concussion and abdominal internal bleeding," he snapped.

I got from him, at least, the assurance that all had been done that could possibly be done to save the boy.

"Was he conscious at all—after the accident?"

"Impossible!" came the emphatic reply.

"Where is he, now?" I asked.

A nurse took me to a back entrance of the hospital where an undertaker was waiting for me. The body was in the back of his station wagon, lying on a stretcher.

I looked at the boy's dear face and turned to the nurse, "Yes, that's my son," I told her.

Then I bent over and kissed him. His hair still had that living, heavy, matted feeling I knew so well from years of affection between us. His face was as strikingly handsome in death as in life. I stood with my hands on the tailgate of the station wagon until a spasm of pain had passed. Then I gave the undertaker the name of a funeral director in our home town of Rye, New York, forty-five minutes from New York City.

When I reached the entrance to the hospital again, I found Paul Wright there with Paul Abry. Mr. Wright was one of Peter's favorite teachers, a member of Groton's faculty for almost forty years. He had driven all the way from Maine for that brief meeting!

Later I drove to the state troopers' headquarters. My

chief concern now was to find the place where the accident had occurred. The officer at the desk turned out to be the son of a Baptist minister I once knew in Albany.

"Could you direct me to the place where it happened?" I asked.

"If you can wait until I go off duty in a few minutes, I'll take you myself."

We went in his car. And then, there it was: the wrecked car and my son's blood on a tree. The trooper, sensitive to my shock, showed me the deep track in the sandy soil by the road, the broken axle of the car, trying so valiantly to assuage my grief by assuring me that accidents like this were not uncommon. He even suggested that the wheel track indicated that Peter had swerved the car abruptly to the left to avoid hitting another tree to the right. Without that sharp turn to the left the other passengers would have taken the impact of the collision. I kept staring at the demolished car, so empty and quiet.

"Thank you, George," was all I was able to murmur as we drove back to headquarters.

Then I headed for home.

The sky was just beginning to darken as I turned my car into the long dirt road. Rosa, our beloved cook, met me at the door. She put her arms around me saying over and over again, "Oh, misery, misery, misery." The word was pronounced in three long syllables, *miz-er-eee*. It was a channel. My feelings flowed through her intonation, blended with her sympathy, became one with the long, long river of human woe.

The children were very quiet as I outlined the arrangements. "We'll have the funeral in the church in Rye, day after tomorrow," I said. I glanced out at the water.

"Carola, come with me for a swim—please?"

We changed into our swim suits; pushed our rowboat from the dock; and soon we were on the other side of the pond, walking hand in hand across the sandbar toward the washing of the surf. We had neither of us said a word since leaving the porch. We dropped our towels on the sand and walked slowly toward the place where the waves were breaking on the beach. I was in the water first. She waited for me to turn and look back before she dove into the next roll of waves.

In a minute we were swimming side by side, using the Australian crawl stroke we both knew so well. We swam perhaps a hundred strokes, then floated to catch our breaths before swimming back to the shore. As we waded out of the water our hands caught and at the edge of the sea, just beyond the curl of the waves, we embraced, holding each other in a fierce attempt to stop the dawn of our inward turmoil. It was no use. After the rush of feeling had passed, we hugged our towels about us, seated on the sand with our legs pulled up and resting our arms on our knees. And there I told her every detail of the day that I could remember.

It was dark as we tied the painter of the rowboat to the cleat of the dock and climbed the hill back to our house. Timothy had started a fire in the fireplace. We ate what we could of Rosa's fried chicken; and I talked about the day to the children.

Every fact was important: the broken axle, the sandy

soil, the swerve in the ground, the doctor's certainty that he had not regained consciousness, the other young people in the car, the undertaker's role, the transfer of the body from New Hampshire to New York. These were the bricks and mortar with which our minds began to build the structure of a monumental fact we could scarcely believe: Peter was dead. We were faced with its suddenness and its irrevocability, and the fingers of our minds reached out for details which would help us accommodate the unbelievable.

The funeral was an unforgettably beautiful occasion. Carola, the children and I sat together in the front pew. There at the foot of the chancel steps a few feet away was the coffin, covered by the church pall, a golden-threaded cloth with a fair blue cross down the length of it. That pall comforted me. The thought of the crucified arms of Christ enfolding our son stirred my deepest faith.

The church was packed. Almost all of Peter's classmates from Groton were there, singing the old hymns with their vigorous young male voices. At the end, John Crocker, Groton's headmaster, lifted his hands over the boy and prayed: "Unto Almighty God who created you, we commit you; unto Christ Jesus who saved you, we commit you; and unto the Holy Spirit who sanctified you, we commit you." Afterwards friends poured through our home next door.

The following day the family and I buried him in a plot of green earth with seven generations of his forebears, beginning with Charles McKnight, M.D., Surgeon General under George Washington.

✝

It is now ten years since I walked away from that hillside near Poughkeepsie, New York. I have found the battle of grief a constant one. The cup has had to be accepted not once only at the beginning, though that first time was the most decisive one, but over and over again; saying to myself each time, "Be willing to have it so." The temptation to run away from such pain is great, but I have learned that perseverance in reality will bring me, time and again, to the feet of Him who is Reality.

Unexpectedly, something will open old wounds. It may be an anniversary, a piece of clothing, a tennis racquet. Sometimes it is a memory of misunderstanding or misjudgment, and then the knife is sharp-bladed, cutting deep. At other times the game of "if" comes to torment the heart. If only I had done this instead of that. If I had made that decision instead of this one. If only I hadn't let him have that car.

In response to such continuous onslaughts, my mind mercifully pulls my consciousness back to the rails of reason, and I drink the cup of acceptance again. But mine is a stubborn heart, not easily reconciled to that which it rejects. For me the process of walking through the truth has been made possible only by the unique insights which belong to religion.

Were we not so blind I believe we should see a convergence of spirit and matter in the whole realm of our experience. Through the extremity of grief I was brought to see this convergence with amazing frequency.

A week after Peter's death I was walking along the lip of the sea when suddenly before me was a pure white stone, smooth and round. I have never seen one like it before or since. I picked it up with such excitement there was a buzzing in my head. Just that summer I had been meditating again on that mysterious sentence in the second chapter of Revelation, "To him who conquers I will give a white stone with a new name written on the stone which no one knows except him who receives it." I held the stone in the palm of my hand, like a sacred wafer.

A few days later, as I sat on the porch of the Rhode Island house, I was electrified to see a swarm of dragonflies dancing and pausing before my eyes; those creatures of otherworldly beauty, symbolic of a shimmering, unfettered existence rising from the shell of the old, earthbound one. A commentator in the local newspaper said he had never seen so many dragonflies in that part of the country at that time of year. The world is full of the thousand-tongued language of God. Why must we wait for some crisis of suffering before we recognize the divine voice in all things?

One day, several weeks after the funeral, I was in a pit of anguish when a long-distance telephone call came to me. It was a clergyman friend who had recently heard of our sorrow and was calling to let us know he shared it. Then he broke down and wept. Presently we hung up. That was all. No pious platitudes, no stiff or awkward pretensions, just tears and sharing at a moment when I desperately needed both.

The universe is one. The whole order of creation is God's garment. He can use all natural and human phenomena in whatever way His love and power choose.

Carola's reaction, meanwhile, had been to seize on the heart of her faith immediately. To a friend, just before the funeral, she said, "We should say, 'Hallelujah! Christ is risen! And if Christ be risen, Peter is, too.'" Somehow, I sensed then, and it was later confirmed, that these words were affirmations she was making to carry herself through the worst of it. She believed them and so did I, but at that point they were largely used to defend her against her pain.

It was unlike Carola to try to sidestep reality, however harsh. As I think back on it I wonder if my immediate anguish and expressiveness did not inhibit her natural responses. Perhaps she felt it imperative for one of us to maintain some clarity and order in the midst of catastrophe. At any rate, at least in the beginning, Carola rejected the pathway through the pain. She chose instead to concentrate on Resurrection, the many-mansioned Kingdom, the sublimities of our religion.

I thought it was beautiful and brave then, and I still think so. But it was a desperate finger in the dike. For Carola, as for me, the only genuine way out was through the eye of the storm itself. Only, she wasn't ready for that dark road when it first opened before her. She needed time in which she could walk around this horror, take the size of it, assimilate the fact of it, before she could allow herself to plunge into the depths of it. Her faith gave her the time she needed.

Three weeks after the funeral, when we were home for good from Rhode Island, I came into the house one day to find her sobbing inconsolably over a packet of letters Peter had written us from school. I had saved them in a drawer of my desk with a rubber band around them, and she had discovered them as she was looking for our checkbook. The first letter she opened was the stroke which broke the floodgates. From then on we both had to learn the hard wisdom that there is only one way out and that is through the place where the clouds are thickest.

As for the children, they would have to find the way out at a later time. At twenty, fifteen and twelve, their faith had not sufficiently matured to cope with a brother's death, nor were they emotionally ready to deal with the magnitude of what had happened. Doubtless, over the years, each one has confronted his own reality in ways I know nothing about.

But an essential step was taken, for them as for Carola and me, when we all went together to the funeral home before the church service to see "the temple" of the person that was Peter. Over the years of my ministry to people in grief situations I have often been asked, "Do you think we should see the body?" My answer is invariably yes, with two exceptions. One is the very young child. A corpse in a coffin is a traumatic enough experience for any of us; for a child of ten or younger it can instill anxieties it would be better he did not have to bear. The other no is when the body is disfigured by fire or accident. During World War II, I was a chaplain and saw many bodies of young men which were charred masses of matter in human shape. I should not wish any mother to have that sight seared on her memory.

However, Peter was beautiful. His young skin had not been affected by the undertaker's arts. As we stood around the casket his visible physical stillness got through to us, and we knew in our depths that Peter was dead as we would never have known it in any other way. We had set our feet on the pathway through the center.

Eight years later the children and I stood in the same room again. We were there, once again, to allow our eyes to tell us what our minds refused to. Carola was dead.

It should not have been so hard this time, to take that first step of acceptance. Carola's dying had been a long, long process of weakening, anticipated again and again. But although there had been more chance to prepare ourselves, there had also been more perplexity. Memories of tenderness, appreciation, support, warmth, integrity were mixed with recollections of irritability, withdrawal, demandingness and tension.

With Peter there had not been time for the opacity of life to thicken. The unavoidable ambiguities of experience had not yet begun to multiply beyond enumeration in his case. He knew what he wanted from life. He enjoyed it hugely. He never wanted to be top student in his class; yet he never wished to fall below a *B* level. He enjoyed the girls whose friendship he won, and he was passionate about his favorite sport, soccer. And with it all there was an intense bond especially to myself. He was the first son. He was the one who resembled my side of the family more than the others. His mother's problems when he was small made him more than ordinarily attached to me. Our joy in each other was unblemished. This was a principal reason for my decision to send him away to boarding school: I hadn't wanted that bond to become binding.

Though overwhelming, Peter's death posed no ambivalence for me. With Carola's it was different. Our relationship was older, richer, involving me at deeper levels of selfhood—and therefore the pathway through the truth was longer, darker, harder to find. And yet, as with Peter, I knew it was the path I must take. No shutting my eyes, no seeking shortcuts, no pretending that the storm will blow away until I have passed through the force of it.

Pretense will always fail us. It is only the truth that can set us free when we are locked in the bondage of a shattering experience. Not a half-truth, nor a fragment of the truth, but only the full impact of the truth about ourselves: "Behold O Lord Thou desireth truth in the inward parts." But oh—the search for that truth is labor, nothing less than day labor, when the heart aches and everything inside is empty and lost.

My labor was made easier by the generosity of friends who after Carola died made available to me their storybook cottage in the south of Switzerland. There, alone, amid surroundings of surpassing natural beauty, I found my own way through the center. The pages which follow are jottings along that journey, written originally for myself alone, with no thought that another eye would ever see them.

In the nearly three years since, however, I have been nudged to show them, first to one individual in similar need, then another, finding to my amazement that they have the same life-giving power for others as for me. Perhaps I should not be amazed. Perhaps it is when we are most ourselves, most individual and particularized, that we come closest to that universal Truth which unites us all.

The answers I found to my loneliness and pain are not unique—that is their strength. Nor are they limited to the particular pain of bereavement. Whatever the human trauma —whether disease or accident, the loss of a job, the breakup of a marriage, the disappointment of a hope—the way out is always the way through the narrow tunnel of the truth. My hope in sharing my own very personal "way through" is not to suggest that your truth will be the same as mine, but that the center of every storm is peace, and at the end is light.

2

It is three weeks after Carola's death and here I sit looking at the Italian Alps from this *casa piccola* in the south of Switzerland. In the valley below there is a lake whose waters are so clear that I can see into its depths from the second story of my little house. I am surrounded with fernery and roses, lemon trees, gardenias and palms. And though I am alone, the human community is everywhere around me. This wee, up-and-down dwelling is hitched onto a continuous wall of houses, built over five hundred years ago. As I go out I unlock and relock my door in the wall, and scramble my way around the turns of a narrow twisting cobblestoned street to find the friendly faces of those who support my solitude, the postman and the grocer.

The last time I was in Switzerland Carola and I were here together. This time as my train brought me through the mountain passes, I sat alone in my compartment— transported by the majestic otherness of the mountains. "Here I am, like death," one seemed to say to me as I gazed upon its towering, rocky face. "You can't change me nor use me. You can only confront me."

A few minutes later a great spray of water issued from a split in the rock of another mountain, soon to become a rushing, green, foamy stream at the side of the express train.

And then it hit me. What am I doing here alone? Carola loved water in all its forms. In her last months she used to fantasize herself in water: lying beneath a gentle fall of water, or slithering along a brook, or dangling her feet at the edge of a river, or plunging into the ocean at the summer house in Rhode Island. Water was a symbol to her of life itself, of cleansing and renewal, of power which is at once flexible and humble. Again and again in her months of illness she would say to me, "Oh, God, just to sink into a cool pool of water!" Her one last hope was to live long enough to see the ocean again.

I said, "I'll help you to get down to the edge so you can put your toes in the waves."

She replied, "I'll never be strong enough again to do that, but I would love to see it once more." Then she paused and asked, "What do you suppose there is in heaven to correspond to our experience of water?"

Today as I pushed off of a rocky ledge and swam to a buoy in this Swiss lake, there was mixed, muted pleasure in it for me. I went through the motions, felt cooler afterwards, and thrilled to its loveliness, but it had no joy for me. What right had I to all this beauty while she lay dead in her grave at her son's side?

We were very different people, each with marked strengths, each with undeniable weaknesses. Hers was a strength which came from an uncommonly gifted intelligence. She was always ahead of everyone else, including the intellectuals we knew in our married life. Her capacity to sift the chaff from the wheat was disquieting. Nothing overawed her: neither position nor wealth. Only one thing brought her to her knees. It was authenticity. It was that quality of integrity in a person which unselfconsciously reflects a unity between what a person says or does and what a person is. She had an unerring sense for that quality in people. I remember her admiration for a lobsterman returning with his catch, mooring his boat handily, looking at us with those steel-blue eyes one often finds among those who live by the sea. Everything in the man said, "I am what I seem to be." Years later when we knew him better we found her initial judgment amply justified.

Again, she greatly respected William Swann, a physicist and atomic research scientist. The two enjoyed each other. He for her quick grasp of scientific theory, and she for the quality of dedication to science she saw in him. The man was as he seemed to be. Agnes Sanford was another. For this Christian author Carola reserved the highest praise in her vocabulary: "She's the real article."

In thirty-two years of marriage I never knew Carola to tell a lie, and nothing invited her bitter tongue more surely than the discovery of a lie or deceit in another.

Where did such spontaneous integrity and independence come from? I asked her once, and she replied, "You're either born with it or you're not." She thought a minute. "I wish I hadn't been. I guess I would be an easier person to live with."

"Maybe it's got something to do with money and privilege," I said.

"Don't you believe it!" she said. "Rich people lie more than poor people. They've got so much more to lie about."

This morning, returning from the little market on the cobblestoned plaza, I was reminded of that conversation. I had bought some sweet ripe apricots, offering the giggling brown-eyed girl at the cash register a handful of money from which she had taken the necessary francs. I had gone but a few steps toward my house when she came jabbering after me, giving me more change, earnestly explaining with her fingers how she had overcharged me. Carola would have felt a real satisfaction in that incident. Spontaneous honesty was her natural habitat.

A dinner party comes to my memory. The businessmen present were making the usual clucking noises about the welfare programs of our government, exalting the virtues of a free-enterprise system which requires a man to work for his money. Carola followed the discussion until she could stand it no longer; then an embarrassed hush fell on the company as she proceeded to cite figures and facts about the actual percentages of welfare payments going to unemployed men as compared to the amounts expended for dependent children and the aged. Carola was a psychiatric social worker: this was her field and she knew it cold.

Going home she sputtered, "How can people be so sloppy-minded? How can they pontificate lies about something they know nothing about?"

One day, after seeing a client in her consulting room at home, she came upstairs with drawn mouth, tears swimming in her eyes. She reached for a tissue, and blew her nose.

"What's wrong?" I asked.

"He lied to me. What use is there in working with someone who lies?"

It was a dimension of immense importance in our personal relationship. As I look down upon the deep waters of Lago Maggiore I remember a time when our marriage, too was in deep waters.

It was winter. Carola and I were sitting in a bay window of the house we were living in at the time, staring through the leaded casement windows at the snow outside.

"What's the use of going on?" she queried.

"Going on with what?"

"Oh, life, marriage, everything," she sighed.

"What's the matter?"

"Good grief, can't you tell? How could you ask such a question? I'm depressed. I feel useless. I can't stand the children; the house is a mess except when Rosa picks up; and you're so remote and self-satisfied I can never get you to face the truth."

She turned her face toward me and raised her eyebrows. Carola had a vivid, dark Italianate kind of beauty. People were always commenting on her luminous, dark-brown eyes. Until illness took it from her she had a slender, almost boyish, figure. She was one of those lucky people who can eat anything and everything without gaining weight. At the time of this conversation her hair was black, with only a faint beginning of the gray which was to become practically white by the end. Her legs were long and lean, but her vitality centered in her eyes with their intense aliveness of expression.

Her loveliness often caught my breath, even in anger. I answered obliquely, "I don't know what you mean."

"Of course you do! Where are you? What are you feeling? What's going on inside you? What's happening to us? For heaven's sake, Joe, let's be honest with each other!"

Now as I stare at the mist over the Italian Alps, I find the weight of myself almost insupportable. Why was I so unwilling to acknowledge the storms of existence? What was it that made me so unavailable? Fear of intimacy? Guilt? What was it?

Whatever the cause, it created much pain between us because, by her nature, Carola could endure no other way out of a problem except right through the middle of it. I was the one who procrastinated, putting off discussion of negative reality as long as possible, or rationalizing the negative away, sometimes even pretending to myself that it wasn't there.

Money was a case in point. We'd both been raised with the attitude that money is irrelevant. You decided what you were going to do, and the money was always found to do it. Decision came first, money second. Questions of whether it was wise or affordable were secondary. This is not a responsible approach to the handling of money, and I have since learned differently, but nevertheless that was the approach we both took toward the subject in the early years of our marriage. Carola had grown up in an exceptionally privileged environment which she later viewed as a mixed blessing, regretting, for example, that as a child she'd been closer to her governess than to her mother. Money was certainly not that plentiful in my growing life, but somehow the means always became available for me to do whatever I wanted to do, including study abroad.

So we both began married life with the same attitude toward money. However, as the children came and our needs grew heavier, we had a number of financial crises; as many clergy and their families do, we frequently found ourselves against the wall. At this point Carola's attitude changed and mine did not.

It was typical. She would insist on yellow pad and pencil, careful analysis of all obligations, and a plan to meet them. My way was to ignore the bills, let them wait in the hope that they would disappear. And when they didn't disappear I would find some way to borrow. Carola never accepted a single loan lightly. It was always an issue of bitterness. She found indebtedness intolerable and would keep after me until the thing was paid.

When by the end of her life, through the kindness and good fortune of friends and family, she knew that indebtedness was no longer a burden we had to carry, she said to me one day as I sat in her room paying bills, "I'm sorry, honey, I used to be so nasty about money, but if I hadn't kept after you, Lord only knows where we would be."

She was right. I'd been very much an ostrich. She'd

known that such an attitude was bound to be disastrous. You had to deal with the truth and respond appropriately, realistically, in matters of money as in every other situation. The only way out of a storm was through the eye at the center. Slowly, little by little, with her as my guide, I was beginning to lose my terror of the bad-weather situations of life.

3

The longest challenge—the most all-encompassing storm we faced together—began with a tiny lump in her left breast, which was removed on November 22, 1963. Afterwards we could always remember the date because Carola awakened in the recovery room to be told by a nurse that John Kennedy had been assassinated.

Her physician had discovered the growth three or four months before that time. When I say that Carola insisted on facing problems head-on, I don't mean that she went around looking for negatives. Quite the contrary. She didn't even tell me about the lump until October. I think she couldn't really conceive of the possibility that the thing could be malignant. Before surgery she minimized its seriousness by reminding me how small it was. It had remained that way for several weeks while we were in Rhode Island,

and "besides, Mother had a tendency toward small benign growths, you remember."

However, when she was back in her hospital room on that fateful November day, she knew the truth before the doctor told her, because her breast was missing. In place of it were wide swathes of bandages and adhesive. When I entered the room she was still sedated, but not enough to miss the facts. She looked at me and said, "Malignant, wasn't it?"

I said, "Yes, but the doctor thinks he got it all."

She nodded, fell asleep saying quietly, "I hope so."

The surgical wounds healed rapidly and she was soon back at her work as a caseworker and therapist in an agency dealing with marital and child development problems; but there was an inward healing which would take longer.

There was the healing of her identity as a woman, for example. To lose a breast at age forty-four is a traumatic experience. Our appearance is something most of us assume until it is altered by disease or accident. Carola had a particularly difficult time adjusting to the accoutrements which became indispensable in her daily clothing. She said, "I hate the gadgets, but thank God for whoever it was that invented them."

Of course, it was tied up with her sexuality, and since that is where the greatest complexity lies in all of us, the conflictual feelings she had about it should not have surprised us. The worst thing a husband can do when faced with a crisis of this kind is to reject his wife in any way. To touch the scar tissue lovingly, to provide the reassurance that such a loss makes no difference to his feelings, to affirm the validity of the relationship as far deeper than

the physical dimension could ever encompass, to dem-
onstrate the reality of sexual fulfillment as soon as it is
comfortable after such surgery, is to help his wife recover
at the deepest levels of her being from the trauma of
mastectomy.

I wish I could write "I did all of that," but I didn't: my
way of meeting the problem was often to deny it. However,
I learned much, not because I'm that teachable but because
Carola never let me off the hook until I came to grips with
reality. It was not easy, but on the other hand, it was an
unending source of growth because, in spite of myself, I
recognized the validity of her efforts to engage me in my
own truth.

I have no excessive guilt about my marriage nor about
the past. Carola's complexities matched my own. Our saving
grace was that we seldom played the "holier than thou"
game. When either of us tried the trick of self-righteously
projecting his own fears or failures on the other, it usually
ended with a good-natured "Oh, come off it."

Nevertheless, I wish I had been more sensitive and sup-
portive after the mastectomy than I was. I just didn't confront the reality as I should have done. The sexual conno-
tations slipped by me for longer than I like to remember.
I wince even now, watching clouds billow above the lake,
when I remember the night a few months after the operation
when she reached for my hand in the dark and guided my
touch to the place where a breast had been, silently entreat-
ing my tenderness for the scar tissue which remained; and
another night in that first year when she lay naked before
me with questioning embarrassment in her eyes waiting to
see if I still cherished her altered body.

And, of course, beyond that reality loomed another one, more massive, more terrifying still. We could neither of us forget one of the doctors, a round-faced, capable man, who first used the word *metastasize*. Those fateful syllables tolled in our heads mercilessly. It meant that there had been some evidence of a spread of the disease beyond the site of the surgery. We were assured that the evidence was slight, and cobalt treatment might very well overcome the problem. We knew that statistically five years was the magic number; and presently our anxiety receded into the background. One cannot live in anticipation of death. On the first anniversary of President Kennedy's death we read the newspaper account of the Kennedy clan's remembrance of their great son.

I said, "It's an anniversary for us, too, honey."

She nodded and held up her hands, with fingers crossed.

Being realistic about the facts does not mean being pessimistic. There is only one bearable way in which we can meet the major negatives of life and it is the way of hope. At every stage of our battle we looked to hope as our comfort and guide. First it was surgery, then radiation treatment, then surgery again, and finally chemotherapy; and through it all we looked beyond hope to the source of all hope. Hope which is anchored in reality and linked to the Spirit is the most powerful form of courage available to us. It was that combination which brought us through every crisis with a measure of grace.

Today I swam far far out from the rocky shore of Lago Maggiore. In a fit of depression this morning—aren't depressions always worse in the morning?—I decided to climb down to the lake. The sun was hotter than I had realized, and I had raced out of the house in a rush to get away from myself, forgetting my swim trunks. However, there was no one in sight, so I stripped to my shorts and dove into the cool sweet depths of the lake. When I surfaced I swam vigorously for many minutes to free myself of accumulated nervous energy, then turned on my back to float and rest. And there above me was my lovely village with San Martino's straight bell tower ringing out the changes of the hour. For the first time I could see the shape and layout of the town. The place took on perspective. I saw how we are perched on this mountain and our relation to other villages about us.

After my swim as I lay on a slab of rock waiting for the sun to dry me, I thought about perspective and I was reminded of an evening which marked the end of three months of cobalt treatments. Carola had found the treatments excessively tiring. Her depression was abysmal that night. There was nothing I could do or say to relieve it.

I remember going that evening to a favorite place of mine, a chapel seating no more than twenty-five, and praying for guidance about the problem. My eyes fixed on the fluttering candle, I prayed softly and perspective returned. Hope was renewed. Strength poured into me.

Where do we find a haven for our hope? Life never ceases to press forward. By its nature it must do so. Hope is as necessary to life as bread. Where can we preserve our hopes, as glowing embers keep their warmth beneath the ash of my hearth here in Switzerland, or as snowdrifts lie in the lee of the mountainside? There is no abiding shelter for our hopes except in the Eternal.

When I went back to Carola from the chapel it was hope,

anchored in Christ, which I brought with me.

"Honey, we've lost our moorings. I am sure we've let fatigue and fear distort our judgment. This is March. By June we'll be ready to go to Rhode Island. I have confidence that God is going to give you all the strength you will need by then. The surgery is behind us and so is the radiation. Let's trust His healing."

She put her arms around me and whispered, "Thank you, darling. Yes, let's walk out on that."

A simple thing for me to have said. I might have said it earlier in the evening but then it would have been words, only empty words, and Carola's response would have been angry rejection of superficial language. But as it was, she knew and I knew that my assurance came out of a depth we both respected. There was a power behind my words which was not my own, and we both instinctively knew it.

4

In November 1968, Carola was operated on again for "the return" of her cancer. It was five years, save a week, to the day of the mastectomy. The doctors removed her ovaries, and now we began talking about remissions instead of cures. For the next four and a half years we would be involved at a hundred different levels with the problem of an all-too-apparent disease.

As is always the case, our experience was colored by our particular histories and personalities. We were both verbal and communicative persons. We shared a conviction that the most important thing in life is to be teachable to the end. Between the two operations we had sustained the loss of our son, with all the adjustments, anguish and growth involved in that.

Above all, we were both profoundly religious people.

God was as much a part of our daily experience as we were a part of each other's. We rejoiced with Him, we wept with Him, we questioned Him, we worshipped Him, we praised Him, we resisted Him, and we loved Him.

Nothing in our life, nothing in our thought, nothing in our struggle for victory over disease, nothing in our confrontation of death ever excluded God. He was ubiquitous. He entered our conversations as naturally and regularly as the daily news. Verbal prayer was only the tip of the iceberg of our God-consciousness. God was to both of us like someone whom we loved passionately but frequently failed to understand.

The golden thread which dominated the whole tapestry of our religious experience was the gospel figure of Jesus. We read those four books constantly. Sometimes our verbiage differed—mine more theological, hers more direct; mine more emphatic on the Lordship of Jesus, hers more insistent on his humanity. It was a good balance, and I can remember no important discussion throughout our married life which did not in some way refer to Him.

A secondary thread, less all-pervasive but still important, was our experience of psychotherapy. Both of us had benefitted from psychoanalysis, both of us read constantly and inclusively in this field. We did not regard the insights of psychiatry as different from or outside the truths of religion. Rather, we recognized in them the Holy Spirit speaking to His world, as He always speaks, with fresh language and contemporary thought-patterns.

Tonight as I ate Italian food in a small local restaurant overlooking this Swiss lake, I remembered an evening of lasagna and salad at the home of friends in Cambridge when we were living on Brattle Street. Paul and Hannah

Tillich were also guests that evening. He was then at the height of his influence as University Professor at Harvard. Tillich's interest in psychotherapy was second only to his commitment to theology and philosophy. He and Carola were eagerly engaged in a discussion about the growth process by which we are released to fulfill more of our potential as loving human beings. Carola was describing her hopes and satisfactions as a therapist.

"I feel sometimes like a midwife. There are occasional beautiful moments when I know my client is coming to one of those many new births we all experience as we grow. Something infinitely valuable is happening. Such times never happen without trust between myself and the client, but when they happen I feel as though I'm only an onlooker. Both the client and I are caught in a rhythm of the universe, and our hardest job is not to interfere with the pain which makes the new birth possible."

Tillich's formidable large teutonic face, with its mobile features, lit up in response to Carola's dark, gentle intensity.

"I am grateful for what you say," he replied. "But I would not call it a 'rhythm of the universe.' I call it the creative ground. I am not a psychotherapist but I know there are rare moments when there is something present which transcends the limited reality of the thou and the ego. I sometimes call it the presence of the holy."

This was in the late Eisenhower years. In academic circles we were talking much about the open society vis-a-vis the closed society of the USSR.

"I guess I yearn not only for an open society," Carola said, "but for openness in myself and in others. It is what

I spend time helping people to do."

I could tell that Carola had caught Tillich's full attention. His eyes no longer ranged over the heads of the company as they were prone to do in general discussion. He responded, *"Openness* is a most important word. People ask me, 'What can I do to experience God or to get the Divine Spirit?' My answer is the only thing you can do is keep yourselves open for it; you cannot force God; you cannot produce the Divine Spirit, but you can keep yourselves open for it."

"But keeping open takes courage," said Carola. "Perhaps that's what you've called 'the courage to be.' That phrase has become very important to me. I've discovered that as we find the courage to open ourselves to ourselves and to the *mix-iness* of everything, we also become open to God."

Brave Carola! So unflinching in holding the door open to all manner of costly truth, I think that evening in Cambridge she could not conceive of the time when courage would fail. When constant openness would become too painful, too frightening, too exhausting. But as her illness progressed there came times for both Carola and me when the door to the pain-filled reality had to be closed for a time.

As with everyone faced with a life-threatening illness, we would vacillate between denial of the threat and acceptance of its probability. Our relation to the disease was like a highly sensitive barometric needle responding to our inner readiness or lack of it. Now it was straight through the center of the problem raised by new symptoms, new treatment, new medication. Then again it was a strategy of escape and silence, only to be finally resolved by realizing again that the way out was the way through.

I wish I had understood sooner that closing the door,

as long as it did not remain closed, was an appropriate response for certain times and situations. What misled me was what I had known of Carola herself, over twenty-five years. So honest, so forthright, so insistent on coming to grips with problems, her increasing denial of the disease toward the end bewildered me. I believe now that it was terror—sheer unmanageable terror—of uncontrollable pain, of the loss of reason and awareness, of the unknown beyond the grave. The reason I generally didn't deny the advance of the disease was because I lived outside of it, and the reason she couldn't face it as consistently as I might have expected was because she lived inside it.

She loved Switzerland when we were here together; but she loved Italy more. She longed to return. As late as 1972, when hospitalizations were almost monthly occurrences, she was in touch with a travel agent, gathering maps, books, tourguides of the country around Florence. "Tuscany is holy ground," she said. "Maybe by summer I'll be strong enough to fly to Rome, and we can stay in Florence a few weeks."

It was not as though she didn't know the disease was gaining on her. She insisted on the most detailed knowledge. It was never acceptable for a nurse to hand her some new medication and say simply, "The doctor ordered it." Carola wouldn't take it until she knew what it was, why it was being prescribed, what benefit was expected from it, and what effect it might have in combination with other drugs. On her mother's side she came from a long line of doctors. Medicine fascinated her. She once said that if she had been born thirty years later, she would almost certainly have entered some branch of medicine. Her mind fully accepted the scientific facts of her diagnosis. Indeed, she hungered for as many of those facts as she could garner from her doctors. It helped her, she said, to get her mind around the problem. It also gave her a vital sense of control, a weapon with which to fight against the indignities of it all, as well as fuel for the flame of hope.

This combination of hope and reality was the character-istic ebb and flow of daily life which I learned to accept late in the course of our battle. I wish someone had helped me to see it earlier. I should have bent with the ups and downs of denial and acceptance as a part of a natural rhythm, instead of being surprised or puzzled or depressed. Oh, for a pliancy to bend with the stresses—instead of feeling I always have to combat them or control them! I didn't see this alternation between acceptance and denial as Carola's natural stride until almost the end. I should have caught it long before. After the mastectomy she gave me the clue to combining the two responses creatively, but I missed it. It was during the radiation treatment.

She explained to me how the precise area of treatment was marked on her chest ahead of time, and how she felt as she lay on the hard table awaiting the brief interval of radiation. She said, "As I lie there I think of the radiation beam as a command of God speaking to His creation, com-manding the cells of my body to cooperate with one another as He designed them to do." It was a wonderful combina-tion of fact and hope. There was no glossing over of the harsh realities, yet they were caught up into her imagination and used by her faith.

Carola was totally different from a man I recently buried who never once asked his doctor for the truth. Those nearest to him were agreed that he didn't want to know the facts. I visited him almost daily during the last weeks of his battle with carcinoma of the esophagus. Like any pastor I am frequently involved with terminal illness, with the aid of prayer and faith helping the patient to come to terms with his situation. But try as I did, I could never find an opening with this man to share the truth with him. To everyone, even within hours of his death, he insisted upon minimizing his condition as an obstruction in his throat which would be treated in some effective way. He sat on the edge of his bed, gasping for breath, a skeleton, so weak he could not stand up, yet he insisted it was a temporary "virus" and he would get on top of it in another week.

I think we should not dismiss this attitude lightly. It is one way of meeting a life-threatening crisis. Some people choose it, even though in their secret hearts they recognize that death is near, because they know their particular families and become convinced it is the simplest and least burdensome way in which to meet the issue. It is a response which is not without its validity in certain cases, but I always regret it, for an incomparable opportunity for love and sharing is missed. At its root many people choose this option because they cannot face the law of life's incompleteness. Their lack of fulfillment may have been major, radically denying them much of what is most beautiful in life. For such persons, death is the final betrayal, not to be admitted, else we should be left with only the tatters of life's treasures in our hands. These agree with Walt Whitman when he said, "Living is the little that is left over from dying."

Someone close to my friend, after she learned the true

diagnosis, asked me, "Don't you think we should urge the doctor to tell him what he's got?"

I said, "No, please let's not do that." I believe that, in spite of my reservations about it. The patient should always set the pace. If he doesn't respond to sensitively phrased questions, within the context of a relationship of trust, by showing that he knows the truth and wants to discuss it, no outsider, not even the doctor or the spouse, should take it upon himself to choose it otherwise. To do so is to brutalize the patient, to overwhelm his privacy, to make decisions for him which he has already made in other ways.

But how much potential help and healing, what chances for God's intervention in our lives, we lose when we shut the door permanently to the truth! I remember a conversation I had with a man whose company folded just before I left for Switzerland. Work for most of us is bound up with all that we think of ourselves, with how we relate to people, with security and health. I know this man will come out of joblessness a better person. He didn't minimize the problem nor did he deny his feelings about it. He freely confessed his panic, his emptiness, his fear of failure, his worry about the future, his children, his wife. It was all out there before us as we talked quietly, honestly. Then he began analyzing his alternatives: unemployment insurance, new possibilities of employment.

Finally he said, "And I'm not so proud that I'd be unwilling to throw my lot in with that little venture those friends of ours are beginning."

Here was a man who had been a chief executive officer of his company—at a high salary—discussing the possibility of helping a small family-owned company to get on its feet.

The risk would be real. There would be no comparison between the salaries, nor the responsibility, nor the prestige, but he was excited about the prospect.

As the two of us prayed following our talk, I knew the Lord would give him all the strength he would need to weather this storm. His face was set to go straight through it.

Such directness makes me think of Mimi. She had asked for the truth, almost from the beginning. When cancer invaded the liver, her husband and I came to her bedroom to talk with her about how we should share this news with their daughters. Mimi's courage and acceptance at this hour of her illness moved me indescribably. She lay on her bed, weak, thin, wide-eyed, but quite rational. Her attitude was that her life had been greatly blessed. She had a beloved husband. Her daughters had brought much joy to her life, and though she was only in her early fifties, if life had to be surrendered, she was bound to do it gracefully, out of regard for her own dignity and out of concern for her family.

It was so, even on her last day of consciousness at the hospital. She insisted on looking her best with lipstick and rouge, smiling on those around her while never once glossing over the fact that the end was near.

I told Mimi and her husband on that day in her bedroom, "You have nothing to worry about as far as those two girls are concerned. Your attitude sets the tone. They will pick it up from you. They will take their strength from yours." And so they have.

5

After Carola's ovariectomy in November 1968, there was a distinct improvement, and by spring of 1969, she was feeling stronger and happier than she had in months. We gave God our thanks, and praised Him for modern medicine. The rest of 1969 and until the fall of 1970 were reasonably good months. We had fought the monster to a standstill.

Her energies remained limited, however. Extreme fatigue was a constant, nagging irritant that we learned to live with, never gracefully, but adequately. Throughout those two years, though the anxiety about her health was near the surface, most of the time it was repressed. She made plans for her professional career well into the seventies.

By the winter of 1970–71, however, the blood work revealed that the cancer in the marrow of the bones had made significant inroads and two courses were decided upon—one was removal of the adrenal glands, the other chemotherapy. The operation was performed on January 22, 1971, and from then until she died on June 26, 1973, our battle was unceasing and unyielding. It included many hospitalizations, weekly trips to the laboratory and to the doctor's office, countless consultations and tests.

During spells of improvement her anticipation of a remission, and a return to normalcy and strength, was eager and intense. During relapses she would be alternately enraged and depressed as we groped our way through to hope again. At the lowest point in the summer of 1971 when her pain and debilitation were severe, there was a time when her acceptance of death opened new avenues of communion and love between us, renewing and refreshing the springs of a long and loyal love. Then her strength gathered ever so slowly, but steadily, and we were filled with new hope and joy.

Her improvement at that time enabled us to go to our summer house in Rhode Island for a few days. As I knelt on the floor applying grey paint to the large front porch, Carola read aloud to me Isak Dinesen's *Out of Africa*. However, when we returned from Rhode Island, she was so weak that I questioned the wisdom of having made the trip.

Why Carola did not die in 1971 is an unanswerable question in the minds of many associated with her treatment. My own conclusion is that prayer and medicine achieved a precarious balance of forces which carried us through another ten months before the disease gained on us once more. "A standoff" the medical profession calls it. That plateau was obtained by January of 1972 and persisted at about the same level until October. From October

1972 until May 1973, we were faced with short hospitalizations every month and steady deterioration. On May 21,
1973, Carola entered the hospital for the last time.

I have taken the trouble to spell out the dates involved
because the span of time is a relevant factor in all that we
learned and suffered. We should not have learned so much
if death had come in the summer of 1971. I am convinced
time is one of the few pluses in cancer.

I used to ask myself in those last two years of so much
pain and turmoil, What is the use of this? What is the purpose of it all? Why doesn't God release her? These questions
are bound to arise, but though irresistible, they are useless.
The answers will only be found, if ever, after it is all over;
and even those we find are partial.

I am sure I am not untypical. One of the feelings which
confused and troubled me most at this time of constant
demand, weakness, crazy swings between elation and depression, was the hope in me that it might end soon. There
were so many friends praying for health, affirming her
healing, how could I be a block to their efforts by hoping
she would be quickly delivered from her anguish? I knew,
too, that my wish was partly selfish. I was drained almost
beyond endurance.

Yesterday as I lay floating on the surface of Lago Maggiore, I thought of that summer of exhaustion and I thought
of a neighbor's pool in Rye where I swam often in those
hot weeks of '72. I used to lie on my back in the water,
watch the clouds drifting above me, and pray over and over
again, "Release—Release—Release."

By the fall, though, I had come to my senses and realized
I shouldn't get ahead of where Carola was. "I must not pace

myself ahead of her nor behind her, but walk at her side where she is," I told myself repeatedly. "Don't overguess the course of things. Be content to take them one day at a time." But the dear God knows how much easier that is to tell oneself than it is to do it when the suffering is great.

At this time we started a new medication. Carola had high hopes from it and I felt like a traitor if I did not join her hopes wholeheartedly, fighting every inch of the way with her. After awhile, however, as I say, I learned to flow with the course of the disease, giving up any occupation on my part with the ultimate issue and meeting each turn in the battle as it came. To deal with it in any total frame of reference was only confusing and debilitating for me. Again, I had to find my own resources of strength and comfort and meet each day as it came, each stage as it was, surrendering any need in me to shape what I was utterly powerless to control anyhow. Such a conclusion opened doors of new patience and strength for me.

It was the last autumn of her life. We fulfilled a dream we had plotted and planned for weeks. We travelled north to New Hampshire to see the gold and red of the mountains. We located a charming small lodge, with rooms available on the ground floor. Our windows looked out to the White Mountain range; the air was sweet and clear; the mountains were in a full chorus of brilliant praise. I fetched breakfast from the dining room on a tray each morning, and about 10 o'clock we set out in our car to explore all the mountain trails on which an automobile could pass. Again and again we found ourselves deep in the woods, at the edge of a flowing stream. She didn't have the strength to walk to the water as she wished to do, so she sat in the car with her arms folded on the edge of the window. Resting her chin on her arms, she would breathe the air, speaking only in whispers in order not to miss a single sound of the woods or the gurgling of the water, saying over and over again, "It is *so* beautiful."

All of her life she had loved the Connecticut River. She and I had often seen the place in Saybrook where the river finally flows into the sea, but we had never seen where it begins high in the mountains of New Hampshire. One day during this lovely week we determined to find the source. Where did the river rise?

Thanks to her skill in reading maps, and the guidance of a local friend, we wound up and up in our green Pontiac until the road grew too narrow to go farther. There she insisted on getting out, and by easy stages, her weight on me, we found it. She lay on her tummy and drank from the tiny stream, pushing her face into the freshness of it. It was a sweet moment of pure victory.

Then she rolled to her side and was alarmed to realize she couldn't get up. I lay down beside her. We embraced face-to-face. She said, "I wish I could die right here, in your arms." In a moment she added, "In the mountains where the streams of living water flow." We made a pillow of my jacket and lay by the stream for a stretch of time.

Presently I suggested she put her hands and elbows on my back so I could lift her to her knees. Then she put her arms around my neck, holding me piggy-back while I gradually stood upright. Clinging to each other like this we struggled back to the car.

"It was worth it," she sighed.

I can remember now the things I thought about that day

as I held her in my arms. The smell of the lemon tree in my garden here in the Tessin is bittersweet like those recollections.

I said, "Forgive me, darling, for all my mulishness and stubbornness and distance and withdrawnness and refusal to communicate."

"I don't like the word *forgiveness,*" she responded.

"Why not?"

"Well, the person who forgives is bound to feel superior, and the person who is forgiven is bound to feel humiliated, and I don't think either one fits us."

"Then what word would you use?"

"I'd rather say, 'Beloved, it's nobody's fault. It's all right and I understand.' " She turned her head on our tweedy pillow to look directly into my eyes when she said that. I knew she meant it as something I was to remember.

What a long path it had been from the time when we fell in love in Chicago to that day beside a whispering stream in the White Mountains. Yet somehow the end was like the beginning. T. S. Eliot was right—the beginning and the end are mysteriously interconnected.

We had a wild and tumultuous beginning. We were both twenty-three. She had finished graduate school, I had four months to go in seminary when we were married. My sister and a mutual friend had been the agents of our meeting. We began dating at once: dancing, nightclubs, dinner, theater, the Chicago Symphony, the Art Institute, long walks along Michigan Avenue, deep talk, frivolous talk.

We passionately desired one another, but without ever talking of it we reserved sexual union until after marriage. We were deliriously happy. We sang silly songs at the top of our lungs walking along the lakeside. Our communication was a torrent of words. And so we were married in the stone chapel of the Fourth Presbyterian Church in Chicago on January 23, 1942.

Her face that day comes back to me now so vividly I can barely stand it: her thin, square-shouldered figure clad in ivory white, her brown eyes huge, her face twisted in a nervous smile as she joined me at the altar, and her black hair, worn as it was most of her life, straight and short, cut like a French gamin, clochelike about her ears.

Four months later I was a chaplain in the Navy, wearing the uniform of my country with pride. She loved to see me in my "whites" in the summer, although I hated the neck-shackling jackets. She got someone to take my picture in them and it was her favorite photograph while I was away in the Aleutians and later in the South Pacific and the Philippines. We wrote volumes to one another "through fire and water."

And when I came home for ten months duty at the Naval Air Station in southern Rhode Island, we cherished that beautiful summer which was our introduction to Rhode Island. All during those brief months we made love as though we had invented it.

Memories—"a treasury," Augustine called them. Isn't it memory which makes us human? Isn't our inhumanity a direct result of our failure to remember?

As I focus my memory on our struggle with the disease there are several memories I can best express in terms of thanksgiving. I thank God, above all, for the remission from 1963 to 1968. Our children in 1963 were ten, thirteen, sixteen and eighteen years of age. By the fall of 1971,

Morin, the youngest, had entered college, along with the others having had his mother for his entire adolescence. From the year Morin entered the Groton School in 1966, Carola and I were alone at home, so that the worst of the battle with this disease was spared them. That does not mean they were not deeply involved. They were, and as the years went on they had ample time and opportunity to adjust to the reality with which we were faced. For their sakes alone, then, I am grateful for all that time, for all the sharing which became possible between each of them and their mother. This sharing was made more profound and rich by the presence of the disease itself. Without the shadow of life's transiency behind us constantly, I think our relationships, and especially the dozens of visits the children had at their mother's bedside those last two years, would not have been so fruitful and meaningful. She always asked the right questions and sought to make them think deeply about their lives.

Our middle son, Timothy, was the one of our four children who had become blocked, for reasons unknown, in the academic process somewhere along the line. He hated books. They represented failure to him, and the whole business seemed irrelevant. All of his life he had been surrounded by a preoccupation with ideas, but somehow it conspired to turn him in an opposite direction. Here in Switzerland I have a picture of him at the age of twelve. His dear face looks so Timmy-like, loving and gentle. What happened?

His age put him in the height of the drug mania which bedeviled his generation's late teens. He was deeply vulnerable and like many of his peers, his insecurities, aggravated by his mother's illness and complicated by the death of an outstanding elder brother, made him a likely subject to be sucked into the vortex of addiction. We fought with him. We pled with him, prayed for him, wept about him, agonized over him, pursued him, waded through lies and deception, worried late into the night about him. Nothing worked: neither therapy nor punishment nor anger nor love.

Then a quiet-voiced, lovely young girl, his contemporary, led him to a direct and vivid experience of religion. He made a full commitment to Christ and then began a disciplined study of the Bible.

"The Word of God says what it means and it means what it says," Tim quoted. He had found authority.

This was somewhat different in application from the authority of my own religious framework. He had found the structure his life had lacked in a daily appropriation of the Scripture. Now his natural talents, intelligence and warmth were released.

When he told me about it, I wept. After all the turmoil we had been through, this was heaven-sent. There was no end to my thanksgiving. Tim had found the same Rock on which to stand that I had stood on all my life.

Some time after Tim's new spiritual commitment, he came home for a visit. He and his mother were talking about her illness and the view of it which Tim had come to believe. They were in her bedroom, surrounded by her favorite books, weaving looms, yarns, a print of her favorite Monet on the wall: a pink house overlooking the sail-dotted blue sea.

As I stepped into the room Carola was asking, "The devil? What has that to do with my sickness?"

"It's the spirit of fear, Mom."

"But, Tim, anxiety doesn't need a personal devil to explain it. Fear is a normal and sometimes healthy reaction to life."

"Yeah, but, isn't there unhealthy fear?"

"Of course, there can be. A tangle of childhood neuroses and adult frustrations."

I couldn't resist joining the conversation. "However, darling, isn't it true that you sometimes have felt a sheer terror that comes from 'nowhere'?" I asked.

I remember her eyes that instant. They widened. She closed them tight a second.

"Don't be an idiot! Who wouldn't be afraid?"

I knew both of us were remembering a night not long previously when she had screamed for me and clutched me to her, crying, "Oh, God, I'm scared, I'm scared."

Tim rescued the conversation. "Weren't Jesus' disciples told to cast out demons?"

Carola brought her attention back to Tim and focused her mind on the problem. "Casting out demons is something I can understand, Tim; I know the power of demonic possession."

"Jesus said to the paralytic, 'Which is it easier to say: Thy sins be forgiven thee; or to say, Take up thy bed and walk?' "

Her face softened. She dropped her arms over the bed table on which she designed her work for the looms. She smiled up at Tim. " 'Tis a puzzlement, isn't it?"

Later on, Tim and I were talking of the problem again. "Dad, I just know God can cure cancer. The devil is trying to test all of us, especially you, and if we could get rid of all this negative thinking and believing, the miracle would happen."

I, who had observed on countless occasions the finely woven threads and knots which tie together our emotional and physical existence, could hardly fail to see Tim's point.

A few times, I can't remember more than four in over thirty years, I have laid my hands on the head of someone and prayed, "In the name of the Lord Jesus, I command that the evil spirit in this person come forth, and by the authority of Christ I bind it and cast it away into everlasting darkness." In the two instances I remember most clearly, the change was immediate and obvious. A quiet, relaxed peace replaced turmoil. The person's face took on a wholly different cast; he stood before me wide-eyed and grateful.

Behind human illness and disorder there does appear to be an evil force. However, I approach the subject with the greatest care because so often I have seen a belief in the devil play into the very hands of evil. It becomes an occasion of judgment, separating the believer from others, contributing to a process of rigid and unloving dogmatism. I have seen such a belief caught up into a web of real insanity, adding to the hallucinatory aspects of an illness.

I've also seen people use a belief in the devil as an escape from harsh realities within themselves or the world. The complexities and ambiguities of life are too vexing. It's easier to attribute negatives to the devil than to oneself. The devil becomes a way around the problem instead of through it.

However, in spite of my disinclination to think overmuch about the anti-christ, I know there is a reality of destruction in human affairs which defies rational comprehension. I call him the adversary, and it is that which Jesus often saw behind the illness and enmity he found in life. Were we filled with the divine radiance as was he, we would perceive the Prince of Darkness more clearly. But we are not, so it behooves us to walk humbly and talk softly when doing battle against the serpent. In the meantime let us not give the devil more than his due. Jesus is Lord. The essential power of darkness does not wait to be broken by the Messiah; it has been broken long since. There is a stream of truth and love and healing, of justice and peace, which is abundantly available to all of us. It is infinitely greater than anything the anti-christ can command.

Carola and I used to talk about this problem at length. She questioned people she respected about it. Finally one day when I brought up her dinner tray she said, "I've made up my mind. I can't believe there is any power in the world which can threaten the sovereign power of God's love. There is more than enough material in the unconscious to explain the cruelty and dishonesty and antagonism of life without having to blame it on the devil."

She sipped her soup, looked up at me and added, "No, the problem lies in our limited imaginations. If we could ever once grasp the incredible abundance of God's love, we'd never waste a moment of our thought on any other power."

6

Thank God for the time the disease took—for Carola's sake and mine and for our love's sake. During the last most difficult three years a resolution of many conflicts was achieved.

Without violating Carola's privacy unduly, I want to describe the struggle. I cannot share the victory if I don't share the battle. God help me to do it as gently and lovingly as possible. From the birth of her first child until almost the last year of her life, in varying degrees of intensity and frequency, Carola fought two constant problems. One was the problem of depression and the other was anger. Her rage could be monumental and her depression could be unspeakable, literally unspeakable because no words could reach it.

Even now in Switzerland I awake in the night and hear

her sobbing cries, and my feet are on the floor, and the old feeling of helplessness and responsibility sweeps over me in waves. Then I am suddenly awake, and it comes over me, "No, no, she's gone." Strange intimations, dreams.

Carola's sister said to her once years ago as we sat together in her living room in Cambridge, "Carola, why don't you control your temper?"

She answered, "I can't."

And Gerta said, "Of course you can. We all of us have to learn to."

But for a very long time she didn't. I should write *couldn't,* because I sincerely believe for her it was not a question of willpower.

Last night I heard a man and a woman quarreling. The raucous sounds came from one of those apartments which looks down upon the narrow cobblestoned path outside my garden wall. I couldn't understand the Italian words, but I understood the sounds of the voices only too well.

I'm told there are professional people around who help married couples to fight clean. I wonder how they do it? Our fights were explosions which cleared the air, and occasionally redefined issues, and sometimes reestablished genuine contact with one another; but they were never unemotional. Carola used to say, "If I didn't precipitate a fight we'd never get anywhere." The way out of a stalemate was often the way through conflict.

In those last two years we never quarreled. We were seldom absent from one another during that time. We were faithfully and constantly available to each other, mentally, spiritually, and physically. That was the major achievement of those last years. The fight-flight syndrome just didn't seem relevant anymore.

I recall discussing all this with her one evening when we came to a stopping place in our reading aloud to each other. That week it was Mary Renault's entrancing *The Persian Boy*.

She said, "Maybe at last, darling, we've come on to more peaceful waters because we've learned better to carry the burden of ourselves."

"What do you mean?" I asked.

"I don't rightly know; but I think it has something to do with the way in which we've been able recently to say yes to our humanness, to our failures and losses, to our limitations."

"Not only our own," I said, "but each other's, too."

"For example?" she queried.

"Well, you've said yes to my need to be needed, to my overconcern for my congregation, to my tendency to withdraw—oh, all the rest of it. I just don't feel as if you were waiting to pounce on me with criticism anymore."

"Maybe it's because I've lost my pounce, darling. But it's more than that. It's a question of acceptance, isn't it?"

"I hope you sense it from me as well," I ventured.

She sat up from her pillows, leaned forward in bed. "Oh, I do. Indeed I do. It's what makes everything bearable these days. I'm just sorry it took us so much therapy and time and pain to get here. Why should it have taken so long?"

"I don't know, honey. There were times when I didn't think we'd make it, and times when I didn't want to make it."

"Not me," she said. "I never doubted deep inside me that ours was a marriage of great validity. We never lost respect for each other, and we never stopped talking for too long."

"I owe that to you. There were times when I would have allowed the communication lines to rot on the ground, but you never gave up."

Today I sat under a fig tree in the garden, like Nathanael in the gospels, and I thought of how, like Nathanael, Carola was without guile; and I remembered how anchored in Christ she was, as she said in a talk she gave in the summer of 1966, when we were both providing leadership for a church retreat.

She used de Tourville's analogy of a mountain climber in the Alps, climbing up one of these perpendicular stone-faced mountains. He describes the rope which binds the climbers to each other and to the experienced guide at the top, and likens this to the adventure of the spirit. Carola stressed de Tourville's point that though we cannot see the guide, we know he is there by the tug of the rope leading us on. "The rope is securely anchored at the top," she said. "We can trust Him never to let us go."

Dependence was an unusually large part of our relationship. The sorrow of Carola's girlhood was remoteness from her mother and father. Her childhood came during the making of the major crisis in their life histories, and their divorce when she was eleven changed her life completely. She was separated from her father and the house of her childhood, which she dearly loved, by several hundred miles.

For a long time she managed to suppress her feelings of abandonment and betrayal. Not until the birth of her own children did the anguish of those years reach the surface; and then it did so with a vengeance. I became the object of her need for closeness; and there began a dependency which was to have much love and hate mixed up in it. No human being feels excessive dependence upon another without resenting that dependence in some part of his heart. Out of this strong ambivalence there came much torture. Infantile responses to it were not uncommon for both of us. Until recently we had a coffeepot with so many dents in it that it was a major undertaking to put the thing together and make it sit upright on the stove.

One day I was helping Carola to get back into bed from the bathroom at the hospital. Her whole weight was on me. We barely made it to the bed. Then she wanted to change her nightgown. She never used the hospital gowns, except before and after surgery. I bought many short silk ones, yellow, white, pink. A small thing perhaps, but not so small when an ego is constantly battered by the impersonality of hospitals and life-support gadgetry. After we had changed the nightie she lay her dark head back on the white pillow exhausted. Then she cried: "Helpless! You don't have the faintest idea what it means to be helpless."

I suppose she hated it partly because it had been such a long issue between us. The memory of our first child's night wakefulness comes back to me here in this faraway place. Holly was born while I was in the Pacific, and when I first saw her she was three months old. The baby-nurse was still a part of the household of Carola's mother where we were living. I wasn't too happy about that arrangement because I wasn't paying the nurse, and I thought three months was long enough. When "nannie" left, Carola got up with Holly for the 4:00 A.M. feeding for several nights; but her energies during the day were consequently lessened. So I took up the task, warming a bottle, changing the diaper, etc. Actually, I came to relish that hour. Everything was so deliciously quiet. Memorial Drive in Cambridge where "Grandy" lived was lovely in the predawn autumnal light. I sat with the child on a rocker facing the window looking down on the Charles River. One day I told Carola how beautiful it was, and how extraordinarily sweet that hour had become to me.

It was mostly her guilt which made her snap at me, "You are so totally perfect I wonder how you stand the rest of the human race." It was the beginning of her rage that she had to depend on me to do something she felt she should be doing. Actually the arrangement was eminently fair and sensible because, unlike Carola, I could go back to sleep again easily and not be worn out the next day.

It had nothing to do with questions of goodness or badness. It was essentially a matter of temperament. My nervous system is just better padded than hers was, or perhaps my defenses are stronger. In any case very early she came to depend on me to help with the children to an unusual degree, to find a new maid when one left us, to help with household chores and groceries, to make friends, and so forth. I wish now that I hadn't allowed myself to be pushed into that much responsibility. It contributed enormously to her rage and later on to other maladjustments, including our sexual life.

I'm a great one for peace at any price, and as I think about it all here on my mountain fastness, I think it was too great a price. I know full well I was a self-pitying martyr many times. It would have been better to have fought it out at the time, instead of retreating into a private world of satisfaction in my work and among my friends. But that's all hindsight, many therapy sessions and many years later. I didn't know then that the way out of a problem was the way through the center.

Now I can only thank God for the time and the grace we had to work through the truth between us in storm and in stress, and to find the calm, the healthy balance of mutual need well before the end. If she had died in 1971, this would not have been true. A great tenderness enveloped us in those final years. We knew, not only with our minds, but in our guts, that we had made it. In the last year, many times I would be distressed by her pain, and she would say, "Never mind, that will come under control. I wish you could know the peace underneath everything else which I feel." Or when I remonstrated because she had slept so little in the night, she would say, "That doesn't matter. I was really quite happy with my thoughts."

Our last summer in Rhode Island we sat for hours on chaises on the front lawn, with bird book handy, binoculars nearby, reading aloud to one another, or talking, or silently drinking in the beauty of trees and the sea, and the light, and the stars at night. Someone may ask, "Wasn't much of that peace due to a consciousness that the end was near, and everyone likes to have accounts settled before it's over?"

Some of it was. Urgency surely played a part in our pilgrim-age those last three years. But looking back on our long labors for mutual understanding and truth I am confident that the serenity and love we found was real, and not some hastily contrived fabric in an emergency situation.

7

Religion played the major role in that hard victory. As I have said, God was always in the background of our communication, if not in the foreground. For us this was not a matter of virtue, or being good, or conforming to middle-class morality, or using the right phrases, or embracing orthodox teachings, or affirming a creed, or quoting scripture to one another. It was, rather, a deeply personal reality which we knew as a constant loving presence, now near, unbelievably near; now distant, bewilderingly distant; yet again before us, beckoning, calling; still once more within us—judging us, changing us, molding us to His purpose.

I well remember an experience of His distance. Once in the hospital, at a very low time in the summer of '71, she opened her brown eyes, which were filled with tears, and in a low voice of pain asked, "Where is God, now?" Throughout much of that year it was a constant plaint of hers that she couldn't sense the Divine Nearness. She was at a loss to understand it. Her need was so great. Why would not that nearness be greater than ever in the midst of the worst crisis of her illness? It seemed like the final loss, the one she could not bear. That nearness had been the substance of her spiritual life.

It was our practice to pray together at night after everything was done: teeth brushed, faced washed, medicine taken, room neatened for the night, pillows rearranged. Then I would turn off the lamps save the one by her bed, pull up a chair close to her side, and read a passage of scripture—almost always from the gospels. After this we held hands and centered ourselves in silence.

I can hear her quiet voice now, "Oh, God, whose love knows no limits and whose mercy is boundless, help me to overcome my distance from you, give me patience to wait for your return, and faith to trust what I cannot feel."

There had been so many losses: the loss of Peter, the loss of closeness to me in our worst years, the loss of her profession in which she had just come to feel competent and comfortable, the loss of physical health and beauty, and now the loss of the Comforter. It was more than she could endure.

Spiritual awareness had come to Carola through her parents. Her father was haunted by the Biblical portrait of Jesus. He had made his own translation of the Gospel of Matthew from Greek and he loved nothing better than to have us visit him so that we could have prolonged discussions about the Galilean. After we were married the New

Testament became increasingly her focus. Jesus was to her the Son of God not because of the miracles he performed, nor because of the teachings he gave, nor because of what tradition had come to teach about him, but because in him she could see no division between what God wanted and what Jesus wanted for himself. The abundance of God's presence in the man of Galilee was to her a foretaste of what is possible for all men.

She said, "He is my Lord and Saviour, not because he was radically different, or a different species, but because his difference was one of degree. Therefore, because he lived and died as he did, I, too, in some measure, can live as he lived and die as he died." She agreed with Kafka when he wrote that Jesus was "an abyss filled with light."

I have brought with me to Switzerland a box of Carola's letters and other writing. I pull one out now entitled "The Victorious Life." It is a diagram showing a winding path, and as in Bunyan's *Pilgrim's Progress,* charting the testing times between where one is and the object of one's journey, which Carola describes in her paper as "acceptance of the sovereignty of Jesus in one's total life."

Until I looked at this diagram I had forgotten a conversation we had in 1967 after we had visited Chartres cathedral in France. We spent the better part of an entire day there, with time out only for some delicious soup and salad in a restaurant on a side street. The organ started to play as we came into the vaulted glory of the cathedral. We sat quietly on some chairs in the nave, awed by the shimmering reds and blues and greens splashing on our faces from stained-glass saints. Later we slowly walked about, fed by the beauty of the music lifted to the honor of

God. Never before had a place blessed us with its holiness in such hushed abundance.

That evening as we lay in our beds we fell into conversation about it.

"It was Christ's house more than any place I have ever worshipped in," I said, "with the possible exception of that Quaker meetinghouse in Rhode Island."

"Yes, I felt that, too; I can't remember a time when God and Christ *together* reached me so poignantly."

There was a pause. We were both thinking, holding onto the day.

"When I close my eyes I see a sheen of color and flickering candles," she said.

Presently, I asked, "How do you suppose the saints did it? How do they do it now?"

"Do what?"

"Discover that state you call the single eye," I answered.

Her mouth tightened and her eyelids squeezed shut, as was her habit when she was struggling with a hard idea. "It all takes so long. I think I'll never get there," she replied.

I couldn't resist the temptation to urge a commitment. "But you could be there now if only you could make the leap of faith and trust you've talked about many times."

As soon as the words were out of my mouth I wanted to take them back.

"Don't talk to me like some imbecilic juvenile," she retorted. "Why is it so difficult for you to accept the necessary struggles of life?"

"I suppose it's a matter of difference in temperament," I ventured.

"You mean your temperament is superior, and therefore

it's easy for you to—"

"Darn it, Carola, stop distorting my words," I fired back.

She simmered while we both recovered our cool. Then, typically, she composed herself and launched into a real discussion.

"I've thought a lot about it. I know the single eye and an acceptance of Jesus is the objective, but 'There's many a slip 'twixt cup and lip.' "

"For instance?"

"Well, first you need a willingness to be teachable."

"You've got plenty of that, honey."

"With my intellect. But it's the unconscious resistance to being taught that worries me. I know I have trouble in prayer groups, for example. I can't keep still and listen long enough, and I can't bear the pious palaver of shallow people."

"Many of us in prayer groups probably err too much on the side of kindness than on the side of truth," I commented.

She nodded. "Maybe it's my old problem of pride and arrogance."

This conversation about the journey of the soul toward wholeness in Christ went on for quite awhile. I said: "It's taken me more years than I like to remember to begin to come out of my tendency to escape from the present by living in the future or the past. I'm always betraying the now with tricks like that."

"Yes, yes," she rose to my thought. "That's what I mean. It blocks our teachableness. For example, our first years of marriage, before the children came, were so heavenly! I've tried so often to bend some present stage of our relation to the shape of those years."

"Another way to put it is that if you get stuck, you can't find God, because He is always in the now."

"You would have to make it theological," she answered, "but that's true."

My eye rises from the page I am writing on. Someone is ringing the bell beside the door in my garden wall . . . . It was a Swiss-Italian girl holding a basket of peaches, white teeth shining in a broad smile.

"*Frutto, Señor.*"

She would take no money. I finally realized it was a gift from my next-door neighbor, brought to me by what I suppose to be the daughter of the family.

That's what Carola and I were talking about that evening: spontaneous goodness, a kindness which asks nothing in return. Our conversation on that occasion ended with an exchange about goodness and the will of God.

"All I know," Carola sighed, "is that whatever I bring to God, He uses, but He can't use it if I don't bring it to Him."

"You mean your talents, your intelligence, your love?"

"Yes, all of that, but I'm thinking more of the web of daily life. If only we would take the time to let Him in between the moments of every day, our times would be sanctified, as you would say."

✝

Not unexpectedly we talked much about the Cross of Christ in the last years. All of my life I have tried to help people to see the suffering of God. I have taught that if the Cross of Calvary is truly a window into the heart of God, then in the most intimate way He shares our suffering, our anguish, our aloneness.

During the war I carried a small wooden cross with me everywhere. Carola kept it in her room during the last years of her life. It is impossible for me to describe the last years of her life. It is impossible for me to describe the comfort she drew from this symbol of Christ's suffering for her. It was always the last thing she looked at before I turned off the light in those final months.

We both of us admired the works of Teilhard De Chardin, the French Jesuit priest and theologian whom the twenty-first century will probably appreciate more than we can. Teilhard wrote:

> Dark and repulsive though it is, suffering has been revealed to us as a supremely active principle for the humanization and divinization of the universe. Here is the ultimate meaning of that prodigious spiritual energy born on the cross . . . a possible Christification of suffering. That is the miracle which has been renewed for 2000 years.

In another place he wrote:

> The world is an immense groping, an immense search. It can only progress at the cost of many failures and

much pain. The sufferers, whatever the reason for their suffering, are the reflection of this austere yet noble condition. They are not useless. They are soldiers who have fallen on the field of honor.

We pondered these reflections as well as many others as we searched for the meaning of suffering. "Maybe," Carola said, "the problem lies in our unwillingness to offer up this suffering for God to use as He chooses—to Christify it."

Someone told her that she should plunge into the depths of faith and thank God for being chosen as one found worthy to bear great pain and grief. She was urged by another to praise God for her plight. Later she said to me, "I'll never be persuaded that I should praise God for cancer. I can praise Him for you and the love of so many dear people; I can praise Him for any valid thing I may learn from it; but I can't see any legitimacy in praising Him for the disease."

Another friend recommended that she hold fast to her faith in the healing power of Christ and release any blocks within her which might in any way prevent the flow of his healing grace into her body and soul. "That I have done; that I will do to the last breath I draw," she said. In fact I don't know anyone in my experience who worked to remove the blocks of old anxiety, grief, guilt and anger as deeply and honestly as Carola did; prayerfully and professionally. I sometimes hear people praying for the healing of their memories over an hour's period of time. They are summoning up a drop from the reservoir of memory compared to the abundance with which Carola dealt.

Of all these various recommendations, made from the

best of motives, the one of offering up her suffering as a gift to Christ in his redeeming love for the world was the thought which was increasingly meaningful to her.

She looked up the verse in the first chapter of Colossians where Paul writes that he rejoices in his sufferings "for you, and fill up that which is behind of the afflictions of Christ in my flesh." She read the passion accounts repeatedly. The prayer of Jesus recorded in the 17th chapter of John impressed her more than anything. His offering of himself for the sake of those He loved became for her a kind of guideline to the Christian life. She asked me for a present-day example. I told her about the sainted Pope John, on his deathbed, struggling to breathe in spite of the grip of cancer on his body, with his eyes fixed on the crucifix on the wall at the foot of his bed, praying in whispered tones "that they may be one."

Then there came the day when she said to me, "I've been doing it for some time now."

"What?" I asked.

"Offering up my pain and anxiety," she replied.

I pulled my chair nearer her bed, took her hand, and said, "Tell me what it's like."

"I've been wondering how to describe it," she said. "It's like a necklace of shining translucent material which runs below the level of the minutes. On the top of the minutes is my discomfort, my pain, my preoccupation with treatment and medication. Beneath those minutes each one has, simultaneously, a shining pearl of pure happiness. That's the closest I can come to telling you."

Later I asked her why she had used the word happiness in that context. She said she didn't really know. That was just the way it felt to her. In some mysterious way she felt that her suffering was being used to divinize the strange economy of suffering and happiness in the world. That was her intuition about it. Her pain was being used. That was all she needed to know.

Her regularity in Christian practices was an important factor in the victory to which she came in that last year. When we were first married, Carola prayed more than I did. She called it her "quiet times," and she said she had learned the value of it from her mother. Soon thereafter the Bible became a faithful part of those times. In thirty-two years she wore out three Bibles, and I now have her fourth one, which she used the last two years, with me here on this terrace overlooking Lago Maggiore. Already it has a worn look. I can't recall a day when she didn't read an Old Testament lesson, a New Testament lesson, and a Psalm, following our church's selection of readings. Sometimes she would say, "Oh, dear, I am tired of this part of the Old Testament. When are we going to be through with it?" But it was a discipline whose long-range effect she found to be incomparable.

And she persisted in these quiet times of prayer and Bible reading even when the felt absence of God grieved her incredibly. She hung on even if she couldn't find anything to hang on to. I asked her how she managed to stick to such a regimen when it felt so empty to her, and she answered, "There's always the Cross and those words, *My God, my God, why hast thou forsaken me?*"

A few weeks after our discussion about offering up suffering, I carried lunch upstairs to her room. She looked at me with a radiant smile and said, "He's back!" Naturally, I knew what she meant.

She said, "There's no explanation. He went away and now He's back again. That's all I can say." This time there were to be no more withdrawals. I felt then and I feel now that the reason for her sense of God's distance was the meaninglessness of her suffering. As soon as she found a use for it, the bolt on her side of the door flew back and the portal opened wide.

As for the moment of the Holy Spirit's coming—for that there is no human accounting. When Jesus used the analogy of the wind, it was the perfect one. There is no other which comes nearer the truth of religious experience. No one can predict the holy moment. When it arrives, it simply comes. We are hushed in its presence, and whither it goes we know not. No one can contain it. No dogma can capture it. No denomination can monopolize it. Freedom is at the nucleus of its energy. Carola said it by using a personal pronoun: "He went away and now He's back."

But her victory had come in hope which did not despair before His return.

8

For over twenty years now I have been deeply involved in the healing ministry. I have always loved my congregations inordinately, and as a young man the pain of life often seemed insupportable to me, as with my people I faced its tragedies. This pushed me to a deeper life in the spirit. I read Agnes Sanford's *The Healing Light,* and it transformed my prayer life. I began to expect things to happen as a result of prayer. And they did, in profusion.

I shall never forget my first experience in 1950 when I knew unmistakably that a divine healing energy is available. She was an eighteen-year-old girl. An infection following abdominal surgery refused to clear up. I'll never forget that narrow high-ceilinged apple-green room at the Ridley Hospital outside Philadelphia. She was terribly discouraged. Panic was at the edge of her nerves. I said,

"Barbara, I want to lay my hands on you and claim Christ's healing. Will you pray with me and expect it?"

As soon as I touched her I felt a vibrant flow of heat and power.

"It's hot," she cried.

Tears brimmed over as I knew the Lord was answering our prayer; it was a life-changing experience. From that moment on Barbara began to heal. She, her physician, and I to this day know that an unexplainable new dimension made that healing possible.

My beloved friend, Olive, comes to my mind. She was an almost lifelong diabetic. Her remaining foot was threatened with amputation. I remember the night before the scheduled operation when I laid my hands on that foot in the hospital and prayed for healing.

The next day before the anesthesia was given, the surgeon examined the foot in the operating room. He told me later, "I couldn't believe my eyes when I scraped the gangrenous tissue away and saw fresh blood supplying that foot."

Consequently, she was sent back to her room. She waited for my arrival with a huge smile on her face. She and I believed it was medicine and prayer which had dramatically improved her circulation.

Of course, there were many times when the results were not observable, for such prayer is not a formula for forcing God's hand. Not even religion can bind the freedom of God. I try not to occupy myself with results. That is God's sphere, not mine. My central responsibility is to be obedient, for when all is said and done religion consists not so much in experiencing God as in obeying Him. My job is to persevere in prayer, no matter what, and give Him the opportunity of using my spirit as He may be pleased to do.

Naturally with this background of involvement in healing and the charismatic renewal of the church, our praying friends are legion. Carola was surrounded with a host of people who were lifting her to His healing light. To the end of my life I shall believe that the remission of 1971 was directly related to the prayers and vigils of these dear people, as well as to the services of healing which I held regularly in our church.

By now the reader will know why those two additional years were so important to us. In June 1973, we were both ready. We were not ready in the fall of 1971. A few months before she died, the chief of medicine at Memorial Hospital in New York, Dr. Myers, said to her: "Don't forget, Carola, it's remarkable that you are here at all. We thought we would lose you two years ago."

Frequently, she would say to me, "Lay your hand on my lower left back where the pain is." I would do so, and in a few minutes she would say, "Ah, now that's better."

Because Carola died, some people have expressed sorrow that in her case divine healing was denied. She and I did not feel it had been denied.

On the night before she died, her lectionary led her to these words in the last chapter of Job: "Then Job answered the Lord, I know that thou canst do all things and that no purpose of thine can be thwarted . . . . I had heard of thee by the hearing of the ear, but now my eye sees thee."

So often I am struck by the poverty of interest among people condemned to years of curtailed activity. It was not Carola's problem. The cultural resources of life had always been food for her existence. Books, music, painting, dance, sculpture: the enjoyment of these things had always been her first line of defense in the daily battle against depression and loneliness.

During the last three years of her illness she took up weaving. The lovely smooth wood of the shuttles, the craftsmanship of the loom enchanted her. She pored over the task of making her own designs. After hours of diagramming, plotting, measuring, visiting wool shops, buying yarns, deciding on color combinations and textures, a variety of stunning objects began to emerge: pillow covers, scarves, rugs, drapes. The satisfaction she found in all this was immense, partly because it was so new to her. She always knew she had a good head but she never thought she could transfer any of that to her hands; in the last six months when she didn't have the strength to sit at her loom for more than fifteen minutes at a time, she was bereft.

Her reading rate was phenomenal. She complained though that she missed a lot, and if a book especially impressed her she would read it again. The novels of Charles Williams and C. S. Lewis she must have read four or five times. In between she read quantities of what she called "trash," mostly mystery novels, all of Agatha Christie and Simenon; the James Bond stuff she regarded as beneath her. "I'm not that desperate," she would say.

Music was another resource. She said, "I'm hopelessly baroque," although she valiantly tried Copland and Piston and Bernstein. Her point was that she didn't have the time to discover their depths, all she knew was that they didn't feed her soul. Bach's B Minor Mass and other classics did. Often when I came home in the evening from calls or counselling appointments in the church study, this music would be filling the house. She loved to turn up the volume on "Gloria in Excelsis Deo" to feel engulfed by the ocean of glorious music. Recently I discovered, unusual for her, light pencil marks under these lines on the record jacket of Bach's "Jesus, Dearest Master":

> Hence, thou imp of sorrow,
> Joy comes with the morrow,
> Jesus is at hand!
> By my tribulation
> Gain I consolation
> Reach the Promised Land.
> With thee near no harm I fear
> Fear not death nor fear disaster,
> Jesus, dearest Master.

Books, however, were her mainstay. About a year ago she reread all of Virginia Woolf, having been inspired to do so through a brilliant new biography of Woolf by Quentin Bell. Then something led her to Willa Cather, and soon she was rereading all of this author. During the last two weeks of her life she read Emily Dickinson's poetry as well as critical essays, biographical studies, letters. She pointed one poem out to me and said, "No matter what it seems like these days on the surface, remember this is what it feels like underneath." These were the words of pure joy she showed me:

> I taste a liquor never brewed,
> From tankards scooped in pearl;
> Not all the vats upon the Rhine
> Yield such an alcohol!
>
> Inebriate of air am I,
> And debaucher of dew,
> Reeling, through endless summer days,
> From inns of molten blue.
>
> When landlords turn the drunken bee
> Out of the foxglove's door,
> When butterflies renounce their drams,
> I shall but drink the more!
>
> Till seraphs swing their snowy hats,
> And saints to windows run,
> To see the little tippler
> Leaning against the sun!

As I reread these words now, I believe that in some deep place of her mind she felt the end was near and was on tiptoe with joyful anticipation.

Shortly after that, she said, "Emily Dickinson is very, very special, but she is mighty thin blood: I need something with more gut. Bring me up *Hamlet!*"

Nature was another link in her spiritual armor. When the children were small she loved to take them on "expeditions" to find crabs slithering before the tide, or observe the sandpipers moving their tiny feet with incredible speed along the shore, or to gather shells and stones. Her Peterson's *Field Guide to the Birds* is threadbare. The binoculars were always on the porch to catch a better view of a flicker, or a nuthatch, or a great blue heron. She kept a record of all the birds she had seen at our summer house. I find that there were eighty-seven checks on her "life list." A walk in the woods was not an occasion for hiking and working up a good sweat. It was a time for quietness and watching, observing the birds resume their natural busyness, letting the mystery of the deep forest permeate the soul. The light on the water, the patterns of the wind on the face of a pond, all of this fed her soul. The last of many books we read aloud was Sarah Orne Jewett's *The Country of the Pointed Firs,* a collection of stories about seacoastal folk of Maine in the late nineteenth century. I read it to her in the hospital. Her eyes scanned the view from her window toward the Long Island Sound, as I read of islands, rowboats, skiffs and sails; of simple straightforward souls nurtured by rocks and sea. We loved the descriptions of sounds the wind and water made, forest sounds and surf sounds. Her eyes closed with intense identification. "I can hear it," she said.

By the end of her life she had become a strong environmentalist, sending modest contributions to the Audubon Society, the Sierra Club, and any other group which was fighting to preserve nature's complex balances.

The last time she saw our few acres in Rhode Island was September 9, 1972. Our vacation was over. We were packed to go home. She stood by the car and let her eyes sweep over the familiar scene of trees and grass and rocks, then across the pond to the sand dunes and the broad vista of the sea beyond. Then she got into the front seat, her eyes swimming with tears, made an angry expression around her mouth and shook her head. I put my arms around her, and said, "It won't be the last time."

"Yes it is; yes it is," she answered as she shook me away.

Friendship should have been a vastly important help, but with Carola it was a more limited aid than the others I have described. One of her dearest and most faithful friends said to me after she died, when we were recalling some remark of irritation which she had made about some-one, "Oh, she got irritated with all of us. You had to fight for Carola's friendship, but oh my, it was so richly worth it."

Another friend said he had been trying to get the right word to describe Carola. *Blessed* Carola he felt was apt, but he had decided that the word *astringent* was closer still.

I have often wondered why friendship generally was so difficult for her. People were easily put off by her. In a paper she wrote in college I find her saying, "People often say to me after they get to know me that at first I scared them to death." A part of it was extreme shyness, covered over by a show of independence and distance. A part of it was that once I came into her life, she found in marriage the closeness she had longed for as a child, and all her capacity for love was fixed on that relationship.

Another element in the problem was a perfectionism which dogged her all her life. She never "suffered fools gladly," and she had great difficulty in accepting people as she found them. If they turned out to be sloppy or unedu-cated in their thinking, stating opinions which the facts wouldn't support, expressing prejudices which she regarded as archaic and destructive, she gave them short shrift. Hypocrisy in any of its thousand forms was anathema to her. Human stupidities, except those dictated by the needs of the flesh, were beyond her usual tolerance.

It grieves me to think about this aspect of her life. She was such a richly endowed person. Her life would have been infinitely happier if she had had more capacity for friendship, and the lives of others would have been correspondingly enriched.

However, here again there was a victory which came in the last few years. During that time there were a few people on whom she learned to lean regularly. These people knew that I carried trays up and down stairs three times a day, attended to the medication, ran errands, took Carola regularly to the doctor's office and to the laboratory, while still carrying a full load of responsibility at the church. They wanted to help with all this—more than she would at first allow. It was partly that she and I cherished all the time we could get together; and it was partly her conflict about accepting help from others.

But toward the end this began to change. I remember the friend who telephoned Carola every evening, filling Carola's life with the rich detail of a busy young mother's routine. Carola's gratitude was boundless.

A half-dozen women came to the house regularly, bringing a flower, a container of soup, a book, a loaf of bread, a phonograph record. Each visitor was the event of the day, and we tried to spread the wealth so that it didn't all come at once. One longtime friend, Peggy, stayed in close touch with Carola that last year though there were ninety miles between them. I remember a particular visit she made to the hospital.

They were reminiscing about days they had shared twenty years earlier when their children were very young.

Peggy said, "I'll never forget Holly in kindergarten. She was the little mother to everybody; and when they took the class picture there was Holly in the middle with her hands folded, fingertips to fingertips, exactly the way Joe does."

"It hurts when I think of Holly in those years," Carola replied. "I was so beastly, always angry. I resented everything about being a mother to small children, and you always seemed so relaxed and happy."

Carola paused, then looked up at Peggy: "You'll never know how much I envied you in those years. Nothing seemed too much for you."

I was sitting with my back to the big window. Peggy gazed past me to the horizon.

"But then, Carola, things switched, didn't they?" she said. "After the children got out of their early years, the tables were turned. You were so much better with yours through their adolescence than I was with mine. I wish I could communicate with mine at eighteen as well as you do with yours."

The talk drifted on to other memories, times spent together, things bright and things dark.

When Peggy got up to go, Carola said, "Oh, I wish you didn't have to go! I need you so. When will you be back?"

"As soon as you need me, dear."

It had been a longer visit than usual. Tears of exhaustion were in Carola's eyes, but she managed a smile. "That's tomorrow, Peg," she said.

9

Long ago I observed a habit-pattern in my beloved father-in-law. We were closer to each other than is usually the case. To me, he was the father I didn't have. His old-world courtesy, his formal manner of speaking, his brilliance in conversation, to say nothing of his various eccentricities, drew me to him. Once we went together to a black-tie dinner party. Not until we got there did I notice that "Neddie" was barefooted. On his birthday he often gave a large party. He would meet a friend in the street and, looking over his pince-nez glasses, inquire, "Will you do me the honor of coming to my house on the occasion of my birthday to hear me sing?" He was tone-deaf, but he loved to sing, and excruciating though the music was, the words were poignant—frequently poems of Kipling's—and the singer totally endearing.

He suffered from deep depression, and on one of my first visits to his house he was nowhere to be found. We finally located him in a honky-tonk tavern, sipping some gin drink and reading one cheap mystery novel after the other. He had a pile of them at his elbow. It was his way of coping with his depression: to remove himself until it passed. Sometimes it took days; no one knew where he was, or even if he was alive.

I can think of many more destructive ways of handling stress. And yet, like all attempts to run from a distressful situation rather than confront it, it left the essential problem unchanged. Neddie never, as far as I know, worked through to the roots of his black moods: to the end of his life he was subject to their devastating and unpredictable attacks.

Over the years of Carola's illness I probably used Neddie's pattern of escape five or six times; except I could never read mysteries with his absorption nor use alcohol as an escape. Biography, not the chronological stuff, but insightful biography fascinates me, and I love European films. There was just once when I dropped out of sight during those last couple of years. It was precipitated by an inconsequential incident. Aren't most blowups?

I had come home about 8:45 that night from a committee meeting at church. Carola asked if I had remembered the facial tissues she needed. I hadn't; so I drove quickly to the drugstore before they closed. When I gave her the box she said, "Oh, dear! That's the wrong-shaped box. I wanted the tall kind. They fit on the bed table better than the flat size."

It was the final straw. Nothing had been right that day. The breakfast tray was unacceptable because she was tired of the soft-boiled eggs I prepared; the medicine had to be changed and the doctor couldn't be reached; books had to be taken back to the library, and the new ones I chose were rejected; nothing tasted right at lunchtime, and so on and on. The tissue box was the end. I quietly turned on my heel, picked up *Eleanor and Franklin* by Joseph P. Lash and left the house. It was a Monday evening. I did not return until Wednesday afternoon. A man can be swallowed up in Manhattan quicker than any other place on earth.

She was strangely quiet when I walked into the bedroom.

"Well, stranger, where have you been?"

"In the city," I said as I sat down, feeling guilty as a murderer.

"If we didn't have that angel Juanita to take care of us, I don't know what I would have done."

"You know I wouldn't have gone away if there hadn't been someone here."

"What did you do?"

"Read books and went to the movies."

"Where did you stay?"

"The Westbury."

"For heaven's sake, Joe!" she exploded. "Why don't you talk? Tell me what's been going on!"

I took a big breath and answered, "It's just that things got to be too much for me. I was fed to the eyes and had to make a break. I'm sorry I did it in such a childish way."

Her brown eyes looked at me long and hard, then quite unexpectedly she covered her face with her hands and began to sob.

I went to her, put my arms around her. "I'm sorry, honey, please forgive me—"

She shook me away and, in a voice which came from deep inside, cried, "Oh, dear God, I wish I weren't so dependent. I wish I didn't need you so much."

"It won't happen again, I promise you."

And it didn't.

I'm glad to say this was the only time I can now recall when I completely dropped the ball in that last year. Regardless of their reasonableness or lack of it, people coping with a life-threatening disease need the constant reassurance of those closest to them. I told myself over and over I shouldn't take it personally when I happened to get in the fire of Carola's resentment against the disease. People faced with physical annihilation shouldn't be asked to be controlled, sweet, loving souls at all times.

The saving grace for us always was talk. I rarely initiated serious discussion about sticky matters, but when she started a heavy exploration of our relationship, potential for growth, repressed anger and frustrations, I was at least willing to talk and to talk truthfully. Before that last year was over I had learned the wisdom of leveling down on a problem and communicating about it straightforwardly. Carola's commitment to truthful sharing had become a part of me by the end. She needed me desperately, it is true. But, as I look back on it, I realize now that my spiritual need for her was no less. My ostrich-like habits would never have been broken without her. Someone said long ago that we tend to marry the partner who can save us from our worst selves. Maybe that's not a bad arrangement.

It is a cold, wet wind which blows in these mountains of Tessin tonight. The wood crackles and sparks leap onto the hearth from the fire I have lit. Above the mantle there is a frieze from Sicily which often captures my attention. In the foreground there is a figure prone on the ground, obviously dead. In the background there are five figures with arms outstretched, fists clenched, faces contorted by grief and rage.

In every family coping with a life-threatening illness there is always a factor of rage to be handled. Often it is buried beneath the crust of custom and convention, but it is there, blazing out fiercely when given an excuse, as when a member of the family fails to show proper solicitude, or else flaring in smaller bursts of irritability throughout the day.

Not infrequently I have seen people focus their rage on God and the question of *why?* I think of the friend who told me about his desperation after his wife's death. He drove his car near a precipice, turned off the motor, and wept his angry tears at God, even cursing Him, asking Him what kind of a God He was to allow this to happen. It was for him a healthy outlet because it was the way he felt.

Carola, however, never once said, "Why should this happen to me?" *Why?* just never seemed to either one of us like a useful way in which to look at a problem. Life is full of tragic and painful possibilities. One of the side benefits to families of physicians and clergymen is an early awareness of this. We learn to accommodate the precariousness of life as one of those facts you can't escape. When it comes in a shattering form the only thing to do is to persevere through it. We found we could do that so long as we had some assurance of God's reality.

Sometimes that reality has to be affirmed by mainforce. After Peter died, Carola put herself to sleep every night for six months, whispering to herself, "I believe in God. I believe in God."

The reality of God was the foundation of everything. As long as that reality could be affirmed honestly, she was satisfied that somewhere somehow the meaning of it all would be clear. Between the options of a godless world created by freakish chance with death making an absurdity of our tortured efforts to grow, and the option of a God whose ocean of love envelops the universe, ever drawing us toward meaning and purpose, she most emphatically chose the latter. But central to meaning and purpose is freedom. In a universe where real good is possible, real evil must be possible too. So the question Why me? didn't beset Carola. Why *not* Peter? Why *not* her? In a world of infinite possibility and choice it could be anybody.

However, such realism and faith eliminated an important target for anger. If we were unwilling to blame God for serious illness or awful accidents, where were we to put down the anguish at those times when our strength was insufficient to carry it with dignity and acceptance?

In Carola, the doctors or an inefficient nurse or a clumsy medical technician came in for quite a load of her anger. If I made excuses for them, Carola would say, "Don't try to defend them; if they haven't had enough training not to take anger from their patients in their stride then that's their fault, not mine." The doctor who was in charge of her case through the last critical years is a great-hearted, skilled, and dedicated physician, still relatively young. At the beginning he was often clearly baffled by her outbursts. One day the nurses couldn't find a vein for a blood transfusion. Her veins had been so badly scarred with so many needles that it was a real feat to locate one without pain. When the doctor came into the room she was cursing the whole process. He said, "Be quiet, Carola, I know how to do this. I'm good at it; now just give me a chance." She composed herself and he hit it on the first go-around. It is symbolic of her victory over rage that in the last year when the technician would come to insert an intravenous needle, she would close her eyes and pray, saying simply, "I know, Lord, that you want this person to succeed in her purpose. Through my spirit help her now." Again and again in that last year, in spite of scar tissue, the IV went in more easily than at the beginning.

By the last year Carola and her doctor had developed a deep respect and affection for one another. "We fought our way through to something good," was the way she put it. The morning she died I thanked him for being the warrior he is against this disease, and let him know that I had long realized Carola was not one of his easiest patients. He admitted that, but said he had learned much from her and that she had been worth everything.

Anger in people faced with death is an appropriate and healthy reaction. We should welcome it, instead of discouraging it. It is the way such a person has of fighting. It is health saying, "Don't give up. Stand up to it. Fight." To concentrate that energy on the details of treatment and medication seems also far more mature than to fix it on members of the family, who "never" call up or who are "only" interested in their own lives.

An unexpected object of her anger was a minister friend of mine who called on her one day. The poor man meant well, and he is a fine person in every way. He just happened to catch her on one of those days when the irreversibility of her disease was forcing itself on her, and she was as prickly as a porcupine. He said to her, "Carola, I believe that a miracle is going to be performed in your case for the glory of God."

"That doesn't make any sense to me," she snapped at him. "Why should I be the recipient of a miracle when Jeanette wasn't?" (Jeanette was a friend of ours who had died after a long bout with cancer, leaving four children, the youngest in kindergarten.) "If others can't have a miracle," she went on, "especially when they need it more than I do, then I don't want one for myself. There's got to be some kind of justice somewhere."

But most often, I'm happy to say, Carola's rage was directed not at people, but at the disease itself. "I hate it," she would say. "I loathe the helplessness of it all, and I'm so tired of being tired."

She would curse her condition, weep over it, cry out— "Why doesn't the hateful thing go away!"—throw books across the room, scream in a rather primal outburst, turn up the volume on the record player until the roof rattled. I have respected these reactions far more than if she had attempted to mask them with a serenity and acceptance she had not yet achieved.

It is not uncommon for the critically sick to feel anger

against the privileged, healthy people around them, for no reason other than that they are well.

Years ago I remember visiting one of my parishioners who was dying of cancer of the lungs. She had tried to face it all with her husband, but there was so much tension between them over a host of incompatibilities and disappointments that it was impossible. One day, I walked into the hospital room shortly after her husband had visited. My friend was furious, her blue eyes swimming with tears. I said, "What's the matter?"

She answered, "I'm so mad I could spit tacks. My handsome husband walks in here looking tan and beautiful from a business convention at an elegant resort, stays ten minutes, and then leaves for more important things, while I lie here barely able to get my breath."

This is not an infrequent note in the anger which spouses may feel during a critical illness. I often felt guilty that I was so healthy, while Carola would be furious that she was the one to be sick. No one would claim it as a rational feeling, but there it is. When two people are bound together in daily life for many years, they can't help feeling that what happens to one should happen to the other. Carola felt an uncontrollable jealousy about my freedom to do things, to indulge in pleasures which we used to share mutually. I remember going one evening to see *Homecoming* with Ralph Richardson and John Gielgud. It was a superb evening of theater. Gielgud's voice and face, Richardson's reserve and authority, were exactly right for that Pinter play. It was impossible for me to contain my enthusiasm when I described it to her the next day. "Bully for you," she said with drawn mouth and angry eyes.

In the course of our marriage Carola had learned to sublimate a great deal of anger. She lifted it onto a higher plane and attached it to larger purposes. Both of us believed all of our adult lives that God judges the Christians of any era not according to how many souls we bring to Christ, nor by how many people attend church, nor by how well the missionary enterprise of the church fares (though all of that is important), but by how well each era achieves social justice. Those who neglect either the personal or the social dimension of Jesus' teachings are guilty of rending the seamless garment we call the gospel.

Carola and I believed that deeply. For this reason she enthusiastically supported me when, from the pulpit, I inveighed against the oversimplification which wanted to reduce the complexities of the fifties to a dualistic choice between communism and the West—attributing all light to one and all darkness to the other. In the sixties I preached repeatedly about racial justice, went to Mississippi to help register black people to vote, and so forth. Beginning in 1967, I began to protest the Vietnam War, ultimately going on a lengthy fast to protest the bombing. I have labored long for adequate housing for low-income and middle-income people.

In all of this Carola was an invaluable partner. She read faster than I did and she had more time to read. She would digest relevant books and articles, bringing pivotal sections to my attention. Before I preached my first sermon denouncing the Vietnam War, Carola read and summarized for me seven books of heavy research on the background of that war. All this was not only of immense benefit to me, but provided a healthy outlet for her own moral outrage. In the last two years of her life she achieved the same constructive channeling of indignation in the struggle against pollution, our short-sighted tampering with nature's balances for man's temporary convenience. It harnessed her rage and increased her sense of purpose to be involved in what Hamlet called the "forms and pressures of the age."

A bird has been hopping at my feet on the terrace. Birds are few in this part of the world; I'm told that the inhabitants eat them. This one reminds me of a minor but not insignificant outlet Carola found for the need to overcome her helplessness and give constructive expression to her anger. At the window opposite her electric bed we installed three bird-feeders, one attached to the windowsill, one to the frame, and one hung from the eaves. Our object was to enjoy the finches, the song sparrows, the titmice, the juncos and the nuthatches. The blue jays and the catbirds were our constant enemies. So we rigged up a baffle which hung on a knob at the window, with a cord attached to it stretching back to the side rail of her bed. By simply pulling the cord she could frighten away the blue jays and preserve the seed for the birds she wished most to see. It proved most effective, and her satisfaction was enormous, because she could, to that degree, control her environment and express her irritation against the noisy jays.

Anyone faced with drastic diminution of strength needs all the ingenuity and patience they and their families can muster to overcome the emotions this entails. This is especially true of strong-willed and intense personalities. There was an angry man in a nearby room on one of Carola's hospitalizations whose commanding voice was hard to ignore. All day long she could hear the man barking his commands, consulting with colleagues at his office, phoning in decisions on everything from company policy to whom to invite to a business luncheon. We learned that he was seriously ill with a kidney ailment, but his physician knew his patient, and he knew the worst thing he could do to him would be to reduce radically the man's usual sense of being "in charge." So the telephone calls went on and on.

Hospital personnel need to learn the importance of all this as much as families and doctors do. Most are happiest if the patient simply surrenders himself to hospital routine and does exactly as he is told. Hospitals are usually under-staffed and life is simpler if the patient becomes "a good boy." But it is blasphemous; it takes from the patient the dignity and control which he is so desperately trying to preserve in spite of tubes, pills, injections and bedpans.

The vast technology of modern medicine has an immense potential for inhumanity, and contemporary training of hospital personnel has barely begun to catch up with this greatly enlarged potential for indignity. Carola never succumbed to these possibilities because of her straightforward-ness and strength of character. No one treated Carola like an infant the second time.

10

All seriously ill people walk a tightrope precariously balanced between hope and despair. Gradually we learned that hopes, little hopes, proximate hope, modest hope, were our primary weapons in the battle. We found it was important to set small goals ahead. Perhaps it was a trip down the stairs, regardless of the effort of getting back up again, for the sake of a bird-watch. I obtained permission to take the car into a nearby Audubon sanctuary. We would drive deep into the woods, stop the motor, and wait for the birds to reappear: once we were thrilled to see a ruby-crowned kinglet. After an hour or two we would return revived and calm. Such an outing might be planned two weeks in advance. Last winter we planned to have dessert with a family we both loved, arriving about eight and leaving a little after nine. That was a celebration, anticipated for

113

days. We discovered it was essential to have something, however modest, to look forward to.

Carola had ceased to hope for a total cure during those last eighteen months. That didn't seem reasonable to her. Though she believed in miracles, and the doctors agreed that there were medical records in which cases of advanced cancer suddenly remitted, she had come to feel that the "monster" had advanced in her case to a point of irreversibility.

Though her hope for a total cure had faded, however, her hope for partial improvement, for prolongation of life, had not. In the last year she had two paramount desires. One was that she would be enabled to be in possession of herself, know who she was and what she was doing to the end. She dreaded a prolonged semiconsciousness, or vegetablelike existence. Her other hope was that when the end came it would be quick. After she died, Dr. Myers wrote to me, "As you know I've struggled with the relationship of faith to healing, and through Carola I understood its meaning afresh. She had a remarkable course for a devastating disease, and although I cannot begin to comprehend fully the impact it had on her, and on you; in comparison to what I've seen in others, she was blessed in that virtually without exception she was in possession of her senses to the end, and her terminal episode was mercifully quick." Prayer answered in gracious detail, indeed.

The week after Easter, two months before her death, Carola lay in bed listening to a tape of the Easter service in our church. She was thrilled by the triumphant Resurrection music. She listened intently to my sermon of assurance that we live and meet again because He lives.

When it was over, she looked at me and said, "It's not death I fear. It's the agony of having to die I hate. The process petrifies me . . . ."

"I know, darling."

Suddenly she sat bolt upright and asked, "What will you do when I'm gone?"

"I don't know, honey."

"Well, all I ask is, don't play the martyr role. Get on with your life. I only hope you have better luck next time."

I knew she was thinking of remarriage. People in such circumstances always do. Some get it out into open discussion, others never can. Carola's natural forthrightness made it inevitable that she would.

All I could reply was, "Believe me, darling, I think I was pretty lucky this time."

No one should be asked to eat the fruit of acceptance of the end until it lies ripened in his own mind, in its own way. One path by which he can move toward that precious ripening is to break the problem up into small pieces which he can handle, one at a time.

A symbolic illustration of this occurred one day when Dr. Myers was visiting Carola at home. It was a Sunday. Her dinner tray was on her bedside trolley, untouched. She complained, "I can't taste anything. The very thought of food revolts me."

Dr. Myers stood up, took a fork and put two bites of meat in the center of the plate, one bite of vegetable beside that, and two french-fried potato strips next to that. The rest of the food he pushed to one side of the plate. Then he said, "Now, Carola, forget this over here. All you have to eat is what's in the middle."

Similarly the best way to handle a major illness is often to partialize the disease and its treatment. Carola used to say to me, "Every once in a while I say to myself incredulously, 'Carola, you've got cancer,' and I can't believe it." True, the endless breaking down of the illness into its component parts could get tiring: talk about the white count in the hemoglobin, the platelets, the electrolytes, the calcium count, the amount of codeine used that day, then Demerol, and finally Levodromoran, the number of milligrams of cortisone used, the phosphate she took four times a day, the swelling of the abdomen, the thinning and loss of hair, the puffiness of her face—all these details exhausted us. Carola used to shake her head and say, "I'm so sick of it all. Let's stop talking about it."

And yet involvement with the immense trivia of her treatment was one way of approaching the unthinkable truth, namely, "I'm dying." It was a way of dividing the problem into manageable portions. Preoccupation with treatment could perhaps be for some people a way of pushing back the overall reality of the illness and its implications, but for us that was not the case. Instead it was our way of partializing the problem and dealing with it by focusing our hopes on the individual steps of therapy.

When I sit on my terrace I can glimpse many mountain peaks stretching south of me toward Italy. As I look back on those last two years of Carola's illness, I can see the shape of our hopes: the big one at the beginning, the lesser ones after each operation—the trip to see the autumnal foliage in New Hampshire, the last summer in Rhode Island, the control of pain during one especially hard month, the last Christmas she shared with the family.

The wisdom of fixing our sight on reachable hope applied to all the heavy issues of life. Wisdom is knowledge of the time which belongs to things.

The night before her death I stayed a shorter time than usual. She was extremely sleepy, rousing only with an effort to respond to my voice. We thought she might come home that week. She had been in the hospital over five weeks and there didn't seem to be much more they could do for her there. So I got up and said, "Well, sweetie, I guess I'll go home. You seem so sleepy tonight." She grunted an affirmative reply. I leaned over to kiss her. She raised a floppy arm to embrace me, and said in a weak voice, "I love you, dearest." Presently, I left.

Early the next morning my telephone rang. Once again it was between five and six o'clock. This time it was a nurse's voice: "Reverend Bishop, this is Mimi at the hospital. Mrs. Bishop has had a seizure. I think you'd better come up."

I was shaken when I walked into the hospital room. A tube had been inserted in her nose and she lay like a stiffened, frightened animal on the high hospital bed, heaving with great lifts of her shoulders to get her breath, eyes open and moving with mechanical rapidity from right to left. "It's all right, darling," I said, "I'm here." No response, no recognition in the eyes. I stroked her head, kissed her brow, whispered love and reassurance. No change. Just that awful heaving, the impersonal look of the eyes, and the sucking noise of the oxygenator. But it was too late for machinery to help. The seizure had poured too much fluid into the weakened chest, and in two hours there was a final heave, and it was all over. Carola was dead.

I have watched many people die. Naturally Carola's dying was unique, involving me at a level of unprecedented torture. Yet I could not escape an intuitive sense underneath everything that it was like watching an unborn infant in the final hour of labor just before birth, the struggling entrance into a wholly new sphere of existence, previously unimaginable.

Long ago when Carola was a teenager, she wrote a poem entitled "Parthenon Frieze." The first two lines read:

> These eager tossing heads with manes of fire
> Seem striving to escape the cold hard stone.

At last the cold hard stone had let her go.

11

And now I come to the last and loneliest struggle. Carola had passed through all storms into the Light beyond. For me there remained the dark clouds of grief to be somehow gotten through.

Guilt has been a lifelong battle with me, sometimes with an abundance of realistic justification, sometimes with no basis in reality at all. Psychotherapy has taught me to recognize one from the other, to do what I could appropriately and honestly do to reconcile causes of genuine guilt, and to see the neurotic impulse which lies behind the tendency I have to play God and make everything "right"— not only with myself but with anyone else who may be caught in the web of my emotional life. It has reduced my rebellion and infantilism. It has taught me to see my own limits, to recognize the boundary where my responsibility

119

in personal relations properly ends, and another person's begins.

I did not come to any of this easily. It involved a struggle to let go and stop trying to control the lives of those I loved the most. I cannot say I have succeeded even yet, but I have made long strides in this direction, and my grief reactions have demonstrated the value of the struggle. I have not indulged in self-pity, nor have I been haunted by unnecessary guilt, nor have I exaggerated my own share in all that has happened. And when I have faced the relief that sometimes sweeps over me that Carola's long battle is over, I have seen it in the perspective of reality instead of distorting it as some fresh occasion of self-accusation. To discover these gains here in Switzerland as I search out my own depth, in solitude among these mountains, is like finding manna on the ground of my terrace.

One of my greatest comforts is that I did everything that could possibly be done. I have no need to play the if-only game this time. Greater still is the certainty that she knew I loved her and I knew she loved me. This was the rock of everything in those last years. It was the reality which saw us through all our years, the stress and strain of two very different people united in marriage, all the normal struggles of two people bearing and raising children and defining and redefining their own identities at the same time. Dear God, what passion and tenderness we experienced!

However, in spite of my comforts, there are the irrational attacks of anxiety. Having suffered twice in less than a decade from the fortuitous dimensions of sudden death and disease among those I love most, an unreasonable fear begins to perch on my shoulder. Who will be next? What will the next loss be? I begin to hope that the next trauma may be my own death instead of another loss to endure. My twenty-year-old son now has his first car. It is all I can do to control my anxiety when I see him drive out of the driveway for the two-hundred-mile trip to Cambridge. When one of my beloved parishioners recently had an occurrence of a cancer in the vertebrae, involving a neck brace, I went home, closed my door, and wept wretchedly. The reactions are out of proportion to the realities. The irrational forces take over. I don't seem to be able to control them. Here in the Canton of Tessin I can at least fight the battle through, where the line of conflict is best drawn— within myself; and gradually a new lightness has begun to come to my heart.

As the weeks have gone on, reason once more is return- ing to the saddle, and together reason and I pick up the reins of my will and, in company with His spirit, gingerly we pick our way down this slippery, steep, winding path to find the broad plains of service and action again. If one lived by his fears instead of his hopes life would be a nightmare. To those whose battle with unreasonable fear is deeper than mine, I can only say that I know it isn't easy, and if it persists, find someone knowledgeable to talk it out with; but, above all, avoid those beautiful souls who tell you that all you have to do is to pray about it and the next morning it will be gone. Prayer when combined with the struggle for real truth is the strongest force in the world; where it is separated from the truth in a facile manner it becomes an empty sham.

Then, there is the loneliness. I wake up at night and cannot believe it is true. My disorientation is often severe;

I hardly know where I am. I see a beautiful thing or make a new friend, and she is not there to share it with me. After so many years one becomes astonishingly dependent upon the other's insights and strengths. Once we were speaking of a couple we knew who had come to resemble one another, more and more, over the years—both in countenance and circumference. Carola was dark, a vivid gazelle of a gal. I am blue-eyed, with a waistline that needs watching and brown hair grown thin and gray. She said, "Well, darling, no one could ever say we look like one another, but I think we've become more and more alike internally." I told her that was one of the nicest things she had ever said to me, and she said it was one of the nicest things she had ever said about herself.

Marriage is the greatest schoolroom of human growth there is, when we persist in it with mutual integrity. There may be people who are capable of mature development in mind and spirit apart from an intimate and permanent commitment to another person, but I am not one of them. I have learned and experienced and assimilated more through my relationship to Carola than through any other avenue I can think of.

When separation comes it is acutely painful to adjust to life without the partnership of that other mind and heart and body. My life had become inseparable from hers. Here in Switzerland, I keep looking at places, scenes, surfaces of water, mountain streams, the sound of a village waking up, the crystal-clear blue eyes and deeply lined face of the old woman who comes to do my laundry, and I can't stop knowing how much Carola would enjoy all this. Or I take a bus up these twisting, winding, narrow roads, with the driver going at full speed, honking his horn at every bend, abruptly slamming on the brakes to avoid another car, cursing the other driver as we proceed with unabated speed, and I think what a lather of rage she would be in, shouting at the driver to slow down, and being more enraged because she couldn't think of the Italian words to dress him down with. The missingness, the ache, the remembrances are countless.

Some people I have known become stuck at that level. They can't conquer the feeling that it would be a betrayal to go on to a new life on their own. Others gradually go on to new relationships and new experiences. They integrate their past life with their new one. I know this is the healthy way for those who have the vitality to do it. I'm sure that the love of those who have died is not so narrow nor so possessive that they would not wish us to do so, were they able to tell us their wishes from the radiance of the love they now know in the "kingdom of light," as Carola called it.

Carola and I talked many times about that next life. During the last two years it was often at the forefront of our minds.

"Who would you like to meet first when you get there?" she asked me.

"Peter," I replied without hesitation.

"Not for me," she said. "I've thought of that but I think it would be too much for me to take right away."

"Who would you like to meet?" I asked.

"I think Charles Williams," she said. "There's something so solid and yet so gayhearted about him, I know I'd trust him right away."

"How do you know he might not be so far down the pilgrimage of the human adventure that he wouldn't be available?" I asked.

"Maybe so, but I do think there are certain souls whose primary task in that sphere is to help us accommodate to the new life at the beginning."

We had both read William Temple's *Readings in Saint John's Gospel* and had been struck by Temple's commentary on the phrase "In my Father's house there are many mansions." Temple says that the imagery in the mind of Jesus when he used the term translated "mansions" was not that of a large, richly appointed, spacious home; but that the Hebrew of the word implies more of what we would call a way station, or a temporary shelter, a refuge from the storm, where we pause for rest and renewal, gathering strength for the next portion of the journey. Temple tells us Jesus meant to convey the thought that there are many such shelters in his Father's heavenly home.

Life in that kingdom must be a shatteringly different and revealing existence if for no other reason than that concealment of truth is no longer possible. We are what our character has made us, nothing more, nothing less; and there is no defense for it. One is what he is.

That is why character and growth are the most abidingly important realities of our existence. One of the truly frightening phenomena of our time is the rising number of people who are indifferent to principle. Facts are things to be manipulated for one's advantage. Truth is made relevant to a given need or situation. Discipline and reserve are regarded as bourgeois. Devotion to the complex painful processes of growth is denigrated as overly introspective. The result is a nation, and increasingly a world, of sandy souls through whom the streams of experience flow leaving no enduring shape or character which is worth the gift of eternal life. They have nothing to bring into that searing unavoidable sphere of truth, and so perhaps their spark of being becomes merely reabsorbed into the divine consciousness. It is not a question of judgment. It is deeply a question of, "What did you do with what I gave you?" as a friend of mine once put it. For those whose lives never escape the wheel of evasion and arrogance and materialism it seems reasonable that death is personal annihilation. For those who take human development seriously, working to free themselves of obsessions, moving into the deep waters of freedom and truth and honor, something beautiful begins to be formed, something enduring. Their lamps are being trimmed and being made ready.

For years I have had occasions in my life and ministry, long before Peter died, long before Carola's ordeal, when I knew in my deepest truth that the veil between the two worlds had grown so thin as to be transparent. I have known myself to be caught up in an intense awareness of that pain where the two worlds intersect. I am not writing of spiritualism or mediumistic communication. I mean a mystic sense of being totally gripped by a power and love which left one breathless and humbled and grateful when it passed.

That sphere exists; I wish to God our generation knew its reality.

If there is one thing Carola had it was character and the integrity which feeds it, and reverence for holiness and the right which nourishes it. I do not have a shadow of a doubt about her survival in the sphere of Truth.

One day toward the end I came into the hospital room. The IV wasn't working right. The nurses were trying to change the bed. She was abysmally weak. She was crying as everyone stood about her helpless. I put my arms around her, got things going again, and in a little while she was comfortable in bed, IV working, and medication quieting her frayed nerves.

"Whatever do you make of it all, darling?" I asked.

She answered, "I don't know. All I know is that God is all mixed up in it with us—all the way." Then she added with an intense voice and a faraway look, "Just think what it will be like to live in a sphere where everyone, everywhere and at all times, does the will of God!"

A little later she added, "Do you know what I pray now every night as I go to sleep? I pray, 'Whether I live or whether I die, may Thy Love prevail.' " We had come to prefer "May Thy Love prevail" to "Thy will be done."

And now as I sit alone on these perpendicular hills, gazing down on the broad expanse of Lago Maggiore, I have felt the Galilean with me by day and by night, healing, strengthening, whispering in my dreams and in my prayers, "All things are well and all manner of things shall be well." I went to St. Martino's Church last night and lit a candle of praise. I had come through.

ONE WOMAN AGAINST THE REICH by Helmut Ziefle

A Christian mother's struggle to keep her family together and true to God during the horrors of Hitler's regime.

WHAT'S THE MATTER WITH CHRISTY? by Ruth Allen

A rural community in the Midwest, a pastor's family, a teenage daughter in trouble—a mother's prayer journal during this difficult journey through pain and anger to forgiveness and hope.

WHERE DOES A MOTHER GO TO RESIGN? by Barbara Johnson

A wife and mother learns to cope with the crippling of her husband, the death of two sons, and the homosexuality of a third.

HALFWAY TO HEAVEN by Max Sinclair

A tragic accident, a broken neck, and a nearly hopeless medical prognosis. But the doctors reckoned without God. . . .

MAURY/Wednesday's Child by Maury Blair

An illegitimate boy's incredible suffering at the hands of a brutal stepfather, and his ultimate triumph when he becomes a child of God.